THROUGH SOVIET WINDOWS

Through
Soviet
Windows

by JOSEPH E. EVANS
ASSOCIATE EDITOR
THE WALL STREET JOURNAL

DOW JONES & COMPANY, INC.
NEW YORK

Foreword

CONSIDERING the difficulties, there has been much good reporting about Russia. The regular correspondents in Moscow, operating under great handicaps, have managed to follow the devious trails of Kremlin policy and the policy makers with surprising acumen. Visiting correspondents, of whom there have been many, have often added a great deal to our understanding of this strange country by giving us firsthand glimpses of the people, their customs and their institutions.

Nevertheless there has been one noticeable gap in the reporting about Russia. So far as I know, no trained reporter up to now has ever gone to Russia with the sole assignment of looking at the Russian economy and the pattern of daily living which revolves around its economic life. Yet certainly economics lies at the core of Communism; it is central to all of Communism's promises and to all the evils which lie latent in the Marxist philosophy.

The Russian economy, of course, has been thoroughly studied by the economic experts and there is no dearth of theoretical writing. What is in short

supply is simply concrete reporting by a perceptive
newsman accustomed to thinking in terms of a world
at work. This deficiency is in no way a reflection on
other journalists who have gone before. It is just
that they went looking for other things.

The articles from The Wall Street Journal that
make up this small volume do much to bridge that
gap. In the fall of 1956 the editors of The Wall Street
Journal sent Mr. Evans to Russia with instructions
not to give primary attention to the devious doings
of the Kremlin or to momentary matters of foreign
policy but rather to see everything he could see
about the farms, factories, shops and other "busi-
nesses" and about the people who live and work in
them.

The resulting reports to his newspaper, now
brought together, make not only important but also
fascinating reading. In the troubles of a Moscow
merchandiser, for example, you get an insight into
one of the basic economic problems of the Communist system and at the same time gain a human insight
into how it is for the people — the bureaucrats and
the customers — who have to live under this system.
It is colorful reporting, but it is also reporting in
depth.

Mr. Evans was eminently suited for this assignment.
As The Wall Street Journal correspondent in Berlin
right after the war and later as its Foreign Editor
and roving reporter abroad, he was already ac-
quainted with the difficulties of dealing with Russians. He had acquired a smattering of the language
and some personal knowledge that Communists don't

mind pushing people around — but will sometimes
yield a bit if you will push back. This knowledge
served him in good stead in his 1956 journey.

More recently Mr. Evans served as chief of The
Wall Street Journal's Washington Bureau and he is
at present an Associate Editor writing for its editorial
page. Both of these posts require a broad understanding of economic matters and some skill at writing about them in terms of their impact on people.

This was the background he took to Russia. There
he traveled some 6,000 miles in a wide semicircle
about Moscow, trying to look through the frosted
Russian windows at the people, places and things
that make up that inscrutable nation.

No one, least of all Mr. Evans, supposed that his
report does much more than scratch the surface of
so vast a subject. But he does succeed in giving his
readers a view of a different side of Russia, and some
of the sights are surprising. That is what makes this
a successful assignment.

VERMONT ROYSTER
Senior Associate Editor
The Wall Street Journal

New York, December, 1956.

CONTENTS

THROUGH SOVIET WINDOWS

1...

Life Among the Comrades

WHAT are Soviet people like? That's a big question, like asking for a brief description of the Soviet Union itself, which is nearly three times the size of the U. S. and currently consists of 15 different nations not counting the erupting satellites.

But for what they are worth, here are some impressions of people, places and things.

The most striking initial fact about Moscow is the unrelieved drabness of the population. You see a sea of sallow faces and shabby clothes, bundles on backs, big untidy string bags, packages wrapped in newspapers, women without makeup and wearing babushkas. And all this right in Red Square, Manezhnaya Square and Gorki St.—that is, in the center of the capital of one of the world's two great powers.

At first it is almost reminiscent of occupied Berlin in the early post-war years. Save for war

1

ruins (and there are plenty of those still in some Soviet cities), here seems to be the same mass poverty, the same picture of people scratching for a living against great odds—even, if you like, existing under the occupation of their high-living masters.

But this first fancy is rather too fanciful. There is poverty, of course, but inside the tired overcoat and under the nondescript broad-brimmed hat you see on the street may very well be a branch bank manager, a department store executive, a factory engineer. Such people are not hurting for money; rather, they are suffering the reverse ailment of not having enough things to spend their money on.

For what mostly gives the impression of equal poverty for all is simply the fact that clothes are of poor quality and almost totally devoid of style. A white shirt is usually a sign of a foreigner, and a man in an American suit stands out glaringly. With women it's if anything worse. Their shapeless dresses and old-fashioned suits do nothing for their figures, and this coupled with the general absence of lipstick makes a pretty girl a rare sight on a Soviet street.

It quickly becomes apparent there is too little of almost everything except government. Nearly all the common citizens live in jammed quarters, and plenty of people live in what can only be described as hovels. It is hard to get used to the sight of these shacks, usually made of logs and often literally sagging in the middle; sometimes they are right next to big new apartment buildings.

What effect this appalling housing squeeze has had on the birth rate is a matter of interesting speculation. Soviet figures show a total population of 200.2 million, about 20 million below some Western estimates, as of last April. The birth rate in 1955 was 25.6 per thousand, up slightly from 1953 but below 1950 and way below the 31.7 figure for 1940.

The usual explanation is that all this reflects the huge loss of life in World War II. Yet it is surprising how many families you find today with only one child or none. A plausible inference certainly would be that they don't have more because as it is they don't have nearly enough room for themselves.

As a generalization, Russians seem rather short, or at any rate of no more than medium height, and stocky. Actually, of course, you see all sizes and shapes, handsome faces and ugly ones, some you would never think of as belonging to members of a Slavic race.

Equally as much variety shows up in personalities. Here is a store executive, loquacious, eager to show the visitor everything, equally eager to hear American criticisms and ideas. In sharp contrast is a cold youngish bureaucrat condescending to "receive" you in his forbidding office with its green-baize-covered tables; there are no pleasantries — you are just something he has to put up with and wishes he didn't. Again at a 180-degree angle is the waitress who gets terribly upset because the traveler "doesn't eat anything" (that is, by Russian standards).

Mostly an American encounters as much friendliness as he would in any other country, sometimes considerably more. If a factory worker or a peasant that you interview briefly seems reserved, it is probably attributable to surprise plus some uncertainty as to how much he should say. Outright hostility is almost non-existent, unless you get into a political argument, hardly a rewarding enterprise in this country anyway.

When you get to talk to men in the upper reaches of the bureaucracy — which is not easy to arrange — the atmosphere is likely to be relaxed and cordial; you get the feeling that they have all the time in the world for you. Also, for a change you see well-dressed people, a man in a brown suit of excellent quality and a white shirt with French cuffs and gold cuff-links. These

people seem not only cordial but competent —
and more candid than lesser officials.

In this supposedly classless state the people
are, as you might expect, highly class-conscious.
It's not only that the upper classes of managers,
scientists and people in the arts get the best of
everything. A middle-class Soviet citizen will
deal peremptorily with anyone he regards as an
inferior, and waiters, maids and porters show no
signs of any illusions about their station in life.
Nowhere is there any hint of happy comradely
equality among the classes.

A general air of inefficiency pervades Soviet
offices. Telephones are left off their cradles almost indefinitely while the clerk performs some
chore or other. Since the phone at the other end
is presumably getting the same cavalier treat-
ment, one wonders how these conversations
eventually get back together again.

Much of the work is done with pen and ink
rather than typewriters, old-fashioned ledgers
and slips of paper rather than card files. Cash
registers are to be seen, but it is the abacus
which is ubiquitous. Many office people work
under dim lights, often without desk lamps.

However, similar offices can be found in some
West European countries. And the impression
of Soviet office inefficiency does not prove that

Soviet industry and arms are anything to
sneeze at.

When you travel to the Ukraine, you sense
little difference between the Ukrainians and the
Russians; though they have their own language,
the Ukrainians are ethnically very close to the
Russians. You see more portraits of Soviet Communist Party Secretary Khrushchev in the
Ukraine, which he ran for years, than elsewhere.

The Georgians, though, are quite a different
matter. Converted to Christianity some 1,500
years ago, they are a black-haired, swarthy,
stocky people; the men are given to trim, sometimes toothbrush, mustaches. The faces tend to
a heavy handsomeness, but you also see fine,
sharply chiseled ones.

These are a fun-loving, demonstrative people
rather reminiscent of Italians. But they also
have a tradition of fierceness; to this day one
Georgian greets another with "I wish you vic-
tory" and leaves him with "I wish you peace" —
a reflection of the innumerable wars which have
crisscrossed this ancient land. Tiflis, the capital,
was the scene of riots earlier this year when the
Soviet government campaign against Stalin, who
of course was a Georgian, first started, but you
wouldn't know it now, whatever bitterness some

of the Georgian people may still feel in their hearts.

Tiflis, deep in the Caucausus with its rock palisades topped by houses overlooking the Kura River, its hills and its vistas, is a pretty town, but away from the main street it seems small, depressed and countrified. Most other large Soviet cities also seem unimpressive as cities.

Stalingrad, despite its psuedo-Greek pillars and buildings on the Volga embankment, doesn't look like much of anything, even the parts that have been reconstructed from the near-obliteration of the war. The reconstruction is in the same architectural style you find in all new buildings throughout the Soviet Union. It is not modern in the sense of clean functional lines; yet it is devoid of the grace or charm of any definable traditional style.

Rostov-on-Don, another badly war-damaged city, shows this same aspect of uninspired reconstruction, though it has many lovely parks and gardens. Kiev, the Ukrainian capital, is also topographically beautiful, with a fine panorama of the Dnieper River from the top of Vladimir Hill, but it somehow doesn't seem busy or big enough to be the third largest city of the Soviet Union.

Moscow is, of course, both big and bustling.

The center of the city swarms with masses of people all day and most of the evening — and sometimes at night it resounds to the thunder of huge convoys of troop-filled trucks and half-tracks pulling cannons, quite possibly on their way to Budapest or the Polish border.

The crowds of pedestrians seem to go out of their way to jostle each other. Vehicle traffic too is moderately heavy in downtown Moscow, mostly government limousines, trucks and taxis but with a fair sprinkling of private cars, almost always the small Pobeda or smaller Moskvitch.

And Leningrad, which as St. Petersburg was the capital for over 200 years, has the majesty of a great city, something for which the Communists are in no way responsible. It was the 18th and early 19th centuries that created the thin spire of the Admiralty that you can see from all directions, the Winter Palace that now houses the famed Hermitage art gallery, the Smolny Institute where Lenin ruled and wrote in the early days, the whole gracious and homogeneous architecture of the city's center.

Perhaps it is imagination, but the Leningrad people also seem more alert and curious about the outside world, as would befit the residents of Peter's window on the West only a few miles across the Baltic from the Finnish coast. In

Leningrad, at any rate, an inquiring traveler is likely to get as many questions as he asks — what is it like in America, do the workers own cars, what does a TV cost, what is everything like.

Stalin is dead and disgraced, but his image still abounds in the Soviet Union. If some portraits and monuments have been removed, you can still find, in many a building, the young Stalin half-smiling with hand on chair, or Stalin having tea or breakfast or something with Lenin, or Stalin the great white father with hands folded on stomach serenely surveying the landscape.

It is doubtful if any other country in the world contains so much bad art per square inch. In the central pavilion of the permanent agricultural exhibition in Moscow, to take just one of innumerable examples, are four garish murals depicting this country's basic "rights" — education, voting, work and rest. But perhaps bad art is the best medium for such a travesty.

There has been some effort to free painting and other arts from the Stalinist influence. But the casual observer doesn't see a lot of evidence of it. In Moscow's Mayakovsky Square just now are two mock-up statues of Mayakovsky; the people, it is said, are to choose which shall be cast. It isn't much choice; one is smaller than the other, but both are in the tradition of Stalin-

ist grandiosity. That, like other aspects of Stalinism, presumably takes some time to get over.

All this adds up to another and not exactly
startling impression. The Soviet Union, with its
variety of peoples and customs under the lid of
political and economic conformity, is a fascinating place — but also a very depressing one.

2...

Vodka, Proverbs and Hospitality

IVAN GADYUSHKIN says Soviet living conditions
are getting better all the time. So do Valentina
Osadcheva, Valeri Gusev and a lot of other Soviet
citizens.

Most foreign observers also concede a gradual
improvement in the quantity and quality of
goods available plus at least the promise of better working conditions. But they note that the
betterment is from a singularly low level. Day-
to-day Soviet life still has plenty of scarcity, and
it's still cut from a drab pattern of state-set
wages, state-decreed work quotas, state housing,
state-planned recreation and state-controlled in-
formation.

To see part of the Russian living pattern,
spend some time with Mr. Gadyushkin, a thin
wiry man in his thirties who works at the Transcaucasian Metallurgical Combine in Rustavi, not
far from Tiflis, the 635,000-population capital of

the Georgian Republic over 1,200 miles south of
Moscow.

Ivan, who is a Russian not a Georgian, is
married and has a son nearly five years old. The
three live in a one-room apartment, plus kitchen
and bath, in Rustavi, a town of about 50,000 specially built to accommodate the 9,000 employes
of the factory and their families. About 99%
of the employes live in Rustavi.

This custom of grouping workers' housing
around the place of work is part of the pattern.
In Stalingrad to the north you drive past block
after block of apartment buildings for the workers of the Red October metallurgical plant, and
after that more of the same for the workers of
the Stalingrad Tractor Plant. In Rostov-on-Don,
similar housing clusters near the Rostov Agricultural Machinery Plant, one of the biggest in the
U.S.S.R., producing two types of combines.

The main construction of Rustavi began in
1947, and the town shows its newness in the wide
streets, and particularly the broad main thor-
oughfare with greenery down the middle. The
apartment buildings themselves do not look new,
though; Soviet construction often appears beat-
up even before it is finished.

Ivan gets to work at the Rustavi plant, whose
main product is seamless pipe, at eight in the

morning and works until five, with an hour off
for dinner, as the mid-day meal is usually called
in the Soviet Union. His 46-hour work week —
eight working hours a day five days a week and
six on Saturday — is general throughout the
Soviet Union.

A locksmith by trade, Ivan finds his exact pay
fluctuating according to how well he fulfills his
"norm" or work quota. His pay ranges between
1,200 and 1,300 rubles a month ($300-$325 at
the unreal official exchange rate). Independent
observers have reckoned the Soviet national average at 600 to 650 rubles ($150-$162.50) a month,
taking into account the fact that between one-
sixth and one-fifth of the working population
makes less than 300 rubles a month.

Usually, a norm is based directly on the volume of piece-work production. In a Moscow
bicycle shop Zinaida Markolova's norm is to put
spokes in 90 wheels a day, for which she would
get 700 rubles ($175) a month. But she regu-
larly assembles between 100 and 150 wheels —
looks plenty busy doing it, too — and so makes
between 800 and 850 rubles a month. Ivan Gadyushkin's work norm, like that of many other
Soviet workers, is greater this year than last.
The norm is about 20% greater for the factory
as a whole.

Even on the farm, the norm rules working life. This is particularly noticeable on a state farm, which unlike a collective employs workers as in a factory. At Digomi State Farm near Tiflis, for instance, where the principal product is dessert grapes, there are 320 workers. They are paid according to their fulfillment of the norm, which is 300 kilos of grapes a day for vineyard workers; the average pay is 700 to 800 rubles a month for the same 46-hour week as in the factory. In this case, if the norm is not fulfilled, the worker gets proportionately less.

And here other patterns merge as well. Talk to Vladimir Akotyan, foreman of one section of the farm. Like the other workers he lives on the 300-hectare estate in a flat in one of the apartment buildings specially built for the farm. So here is an industrial town, a miniature version of Rustavi, put up in a rural setting.

Vladimir has one room with kitchen and veranda for himself, his wife and child (his wife works as a vineyard picker—most Soviet wives work). The flat has no bath, but Pyotr Sokhadze, director of the farm, interjects to say that the reason for this is that construction of the housing is not complete, though the apartment buildings look finished.

Can the workers leave farm and factory to get

another job? Mr. Sokhadze, a big, heavy, square-jawed man in a double-breasted gray suit (not flannel), promptly exclaims, "Kanyeshna! (Of course!) We don't keep them here by force." He knifes off a big bunch of sweet Georgian grapes to hand his visitor and adds that the turn-over is very low. There is a Russian proverb, he says, that a man seeks his own level and stays there.

Actually, a worker forfeits pension and other rights he has accumulated when he changes jobs, and there is considerable propaganda pressure to stay put. But he does not appear to suffer any direct disciplinary measures, as was the case up to five years or so ago.

What do Soviet citizens do after work? Walk around Stalingrad of an evening and you can see some of the activities. There is the Park of Rest and Culture, nicely laid out with lots of trees, flowers and shrubs — a pleasant place in summer despite the fact that the first thing that greets you after you pay the one-ruble admission is a row of portraits of grim-faced Soviet leaders. There is a bandstand, a tiny shooting gallery, a small House of Laughs, open-air billiard tables and an open-air dance pavilion with music from records.

Down Communist Street a way is the Palace

of Physical Culture, housing the sports society
"The Builder." Through the window you see five
girls in gym suits parading around rather self-
consciously and not very enthusiastically. Farther
along the building the curtains are drawn but
through chinks you glimpse young men boxing
under instruction.

But a girl like Alexandra Kolacheva, who works
on the assembly line at Stalingrad Tractor, tends
to gravitate to the plant's own club, or Palace
of Culture. Young and unmarried, Alexandra
lives in a hostel built by the plant, in a room for
four girls.

Anything called a Palace of Culture may sound
grim, but in this case it is not as grim as it sounds.
The Tractor Plant's Palace, completed in 1949,
is big, light and airy. It contains a gym, a 100,000-
book central library, and numerous rooms for
the 18 different "circles" or groups of people with
a particular hobby like playing a musical instru-
ment or painting or sculpture. In addition, the
Palace has a very attractive theatre, with a re-
volving stage; it seats 750. And there is a dance
hall, with dances three or four nights a week, according to Brionislav Alexandrovitch, director of
the Palace.

In Rustavi, Ivan Gadyushkin goes to the Metallurgical Combine's Palace to read, but doesn't

belong to any circle; his hobby is hunting, ducks in the fall, hares in the winter. But a grizzled co-worker, Nikolai Mazin, steps up to say that he belongs to a circle — plays the accordion.

Valentina Osadcheva doesn't go in much for group or Palace activities. A rather pretty wait-ress on the Volga-Don steamer running between Stalingrad and Rostov-on-Don, Valentina lives with her mother in Rostov. She likes going to the movies, especially detective and love and ad-venture films. Some of her free time is taken up with night school, and as she doesn't much care for her present job, she hopes to go on to trade school and get to be a restaurant manager or shop-girl in a big store.

In Tiflis, Valeri Gusev, a 26-year-old interpre-ter at the Tiflis office of Intourist, the Soviet travel agency, goes with his wife to the movies frequently and to the theatre or concert once every two weeks or so; they entertain once or twice a month.

Of course there are also less ennobling pur-suits. Drop into a bar (normally called a cafe in this country) a good bit out from the center of Stalingrad and you find a scene a contemporary Hogarth might relish — shabby people crowded at little tables in a squalid room thick with smoke. In Moscow the city council has shut down the little stands where people could get a vodka on the run, but whether it has done any good is a question. It would be incorrect to say that you see great numbers of staggering drunks on Soviet streets, but you certainly see them.

What's home life like? Come to supper with Mikhail Petrunin, manager of the Red Partisan Collective Farm just outside Leningrad. The Petrunin family lives on the farm in the summer, but in winter they stay at their Leningrad flat; Mr. Petrunin commutes in his Pobeda, the next-to-the-smallest Soviet car.

The apartment is on the fourth floor of a large building. As you enter the hall of the flat, the bedroom is on the left, a coatrack on the right. In the bedroom is one large bed and one smaller one, plus a desk with telephone; there is also a wardrobe, used here as in other European countries instead of built-in closets.

Beyond the coatrack on the right is the living-dining room, with a round table in the center under a ceiling light, a couch along the wall near the one window and a single bed along the wall near the door. In one corner on a table is a small-screen TV set, with rabbit-ears on the floor; at 7:30 it starts functioning, emitting a seemingly interminable program about the life of Liszt. The kitchen, with sink and stove but no refrigerator, is on the bedroom side of the hall; between it and the living room are a bath and a medicine closet.

In this two-room apartment live four people — Mr. and Mrs. Petrunin, their 18-year-old son, studying to be a chemical engineer, and an aunt of Mrs. Petrunin.

In a Russian home, it has been said, will be found hospitality, vodka and proverbs, and that is certainly so at the Petrunin's. Discussing the cold climate and swampy soil of Leningrad, Mr. Petrunin quotes: "God made the world but the devil made this part."

Mrs. Petrunin had short notice about her guest (her husband simply phoned from the office), but she is most gracious and produces a splendid supper consisting of studen, a kind of jellied meat; small tomatoes from the farm's hothouse; vinigrette, a salad of canned crab (it looks and tastes like lobster and is from Baikal lake in Siberia), eggs and peas; sardelki, a large thick boiled sausage; mashed potatoes; bananas (imported, probably from Israel), apples, cookies, candy (Little Red Riding Hood brand) and tea.

As for the vodka, there are three good-sized toasts, bottoms up, of course, but well neutralized by the food. Later on there is Soviet champagne, and finally a glass of port.

This pleasant evening could hardly be said to be typical, first because there is a guest and second because the Petrunin standard of living is above average; one would place him in the lower-middle stratum of the managerial class. But the hospitality is certainly typical, and the crowded apartment is at least indicative of Soviet housing conditions, which for many people are far worse. In Moscow it is normal for more than one family to share an apartment, and communal kitchens and baths are the rule rather than the exception.

What does a person do if he wants to get better quarters? Mr. Gusev, the Tiflis interpreter, can tell you. He, his wife, three-year-old son and mother-in-law now live in a two-room apartment (one large, one small) with kitchen but no bath. The bath must be shared with the occupants of the five other apartments on the floor.

So Mr. Gusev has applied to the Tiflis city council for an apartment in one of the new buildings under construction or recently completed. He doesn't want much more space. "Three rooms would be plenty for four people," he says. But he does want that private bath.

Usually, he says, the first to apply are the first served, but there can be numerous complications; needy people, for example, might have to be taken care of before him. He figures it will be a year to 18 months before he gets his new place. An alternative would be to build one's own small home, but even with state credit that requires the accumulation of considerable savings.

Mr. Gusev's present rent is 80 rubles ($20) a month; Soviet rents generally are very low. In the new apartment he thinks the rent will be about the same, or very little more. His other expenses, however, are not so low. His salary is 1,100 rubles ($275) a month. With his wife's income — she teaches — the family has about 1,700 rubles ($425) a month.

Of this about 600 a month goes for food, about 375 for clothes, about 60 for transportation, about 150 for entertainment. After all this plus rent and taxes, only a little over 300 rubles a month remain for miscellaneous expenses, saving up for a big purchase like a refrigerator, and compulsory bond-buying. Mr. Gusev buys about 1,000 rubles worth of bonds a year.

Like the others, Mr. Gusev thinks living conditions are looking up. How so?

For one thing, partly counterbalancing the increase in work norms is an increase in mechanization and the eventual promise of more of the same through automation. Thus the fact that a worker's norm is 20% higher than the year be-

fore may mainly mean that he has more mechanization and greater skill in using machines,
not necessarily that he has to work that much
harder.

In fact, the government says that the work
week will be cut next year from 46 to 41 hours —
seven hours a day five days and six on Saturday.
Beginning January 1 a new minimum wage law
is also supposed to go into effect; the minimum
will be 300 rubles a month in cities and 270 in
rural industry and trade excluding peasants. A
new and more liberal pension law has just been
introduced.

But the thing most people emphasize is the
better supply, variety and quality of food and
consumer goods. It's obvious there isn't nearly
enough of most items, but it is not hard to believe there is more than there used to be.

An office worker in Moscow says that two
years ago this winter meat, milk and milk products like butter were in very short supply in
Moscow; compared with that, she claims, they
are almost plentiful this autumn. But autumn,
of course, is the best season; what supplies will
be like this winter is something else again. This
woman adds that there has been a notable improvement in the variety and quality of fabrics,
ready-made dresses, shoes and most appliances.

Ivan Gadyushkin, the Rustavi worker, says that now you can buy almost any kind of food in the state stores, not just in the free markets where the farmers sell their privately-produced foods as was the case last year. (But a look at the state stores doesn't reveal any food abundance in most of them.)

A Leningrad engineer reels off a long list of things, from bikes to woolen fabrics, that are more plentiful than they were a couple of years ago. Valentina Osadcheva, the Rostov waitress, spent four years in the Soviet Zone of Austria; when she came back a little over a year ago she says she was amazed how many more goods of all types there were to buy. Eugene Gnydic, a Kiev shoe worker, adds: "I can buy better suits than I could a few years ago. And I have a savings account now."

Compared with the early post-war period prices are generally lower, people say, though they are still extremely high. There have been six general price reductions since the war. None came through last year or this year, but in these two years reductions have been made in particular goods like TV sets and radios, which are useful for government propaganda. Mr. Gusev recalls that brown bread cost 1.80 rubles a kilo four years ago; now it costs 1.35. The government contends that by 1954 state retail prices, including food, were 56% lower than in 1947.

All in all, it doesn't seem an especially jolly or exciting life. But Mr. Akotyan of the Digomi State Farm near Tiflis sums up what seems to be a fairly general feeling when he says: "Every year I earn more and there's more to buy. Sure it's getting better."

3...

The Watched Door

IN STALIN's last years it is said that terror was palpable in Soviet streets. People were afraid to talk to strangers, afraid to do almost anything unless it were authorized in triplicate and countersigned by five officials.

With the uproar in Poland and the bloodshed in Hungary, Americans might think that the terror walked again in Russia too. But it is not so. The Soviet Union has not ceased to be a police state. But as of right now it is a much less virulent police state than it used to be.

Indeed, if the visitor can forget Hungary and Poland, it is possible at times to forget that it is one at all — especially on a sunny fall day in Moscow or a balmy Sunday in Tiflis, the capital of the southern Republic of Georgia.

People stroll the broad sidewalks of Rustaveli Avenue, Tiflis' main street, laughing and even singing (Georgians are much addicted to song);

in short, allowing for different customs, acting as normally as people in other countries.

Also, for inhabitants of a tightly disciplined nation Soviet citizens are a remarkably undisciplined lot in little things. Muscovites pay, if possible, less attention to traffic lights and the traffic cop at the intersection than New Yorkers do, which is saying a good deal. Plane passengers always ignore their seat belts, with no rebuke from the crew, and sometimes even walk around and smoke during take-offs and landings. Nor do these people appreciate being pushed around by minor symbols of authority, such as a restaurant manager telling them to take this table rather than that.

So the picture of a people cowed, mutually suspicious, furtively glancing over their shoulder when they talk together, is not to be found on the surface of life in the year 1956. The chances are that an ordinary man now worries rather little about hearing the traditional midnight knock on his door and being escorted by security officers to the interrogation chambers of Lubyianka Prison.

What has made the change?

First, there have been two published amnesties for persons in labor camps, one shortly after Stalin's death, the other last year. In addition, there is said to be a still unpublished amnesty specifically covering political prisoners. At any rate, many thousands, perhaps millions, have come back. Some observers believe that relatively few Soviet households have not welcomed a "returnee" — which is a pretty good indication of how bad things were in the old days.

Then too, the government has abolished the so-called special conference of the Ministry of Internal Affairs (MVD). This was an administrative court empowered to sentence people to up to five years' forced labor merely on review of their dossiers. It got to be an assembly-line operation. The local police would prepare the dossiers, send great stacks of them to the special court where they would be stamped, and off the victims would go. As far as can be learned, this system has not been reinstituted in some other guise.

Why did Stalin's successors take these steps? The impression here is that they sensibly enough concluded that the terror was boomeranging badly; when a state gets its people to the point that they are scared stiff all the time, it is well on the way toward wrecking the economy. At the same time they could see that forced labor was un economic — and the Soviet Union needs productive bodies.

Despite the comparative liberalization, however, the basic structure of the police state remains firmly in place. "Socialist legality" itself, for example, is something that people accustomed to Anglo-Saxon traditions of justice might well find chilling.

Drop in on Vassily Shulgin, a pleasant former Red Army major who is now People's Judge of the People's Court of the Sixth District of Stalingrad. His tiny court is in the "Two Kilometer" section of the city, an area of dirt roads — sometimes no roads — and tumbledown shacks; Stalingrad was all but obliterated in the war and has 20 years of reconstruction still ahead of it.

The court meets five days a week, handling both civil and criminal cases. The judge is "elected" every three years; Mr. Shulgin has been on the job since 1948 and can be re-elected indefinitely. In trying cases he is assisted by two jurors drawn from 75 in this district. After hearing prosecution and defense in a criminal case, the judge and his two jurors deliberate and render verdict and sentence.

A recent case involved a man who got drunk and robbed a girl of a watch. Investigation began on September 11; on October 2 the court held a preparatory meeting at which defense and prosecution lawyers were appointed (Mr. Shul-

gin says the defendant may hire his own lawyer
if he wants and can afford it).

The trial itself took part of a couple of days.
On October 9 the defendant was found guilty
and sentenced to 10 years. He did not appeal
and is now in Stalingrad Prison No. 1, from which
he will be removed to serve his time in a labor
educational camp. In camp, Mr. Shulgin blandly
says, he will get "re-educated" as well as doing
useful work "in fresh air."

Now perhaps a judge and two jurors, assuming they are reasonably well-disposed individuals,
could deliver a kind of rough-and-ready justice,
in this drab miniature courtroom with its naked
light bulb hanging over the judge's table, its portraits of Molotov and Lenin, its 20 or 25 plain
chairs for spectators, and its defendant's dock.

Still, the reliance of our drunken robber, as
he sat in that cage, had to be wholly on the opinion of three men — and for all practical purposes
that of one man, the judge. The distance from
this kind of tribunal to the presumably defunct
court of the MVD does not seem very great.

To see another pillar of the police state, consider the administration of apartment buildings.
In Stalingrad there is a special administrator for
every five or six apartment houses. In Moscow,
according to a native of that city, there may be

one administrator for just one large building.
Whatever the local variations, the system itself
is found throughout the Soviet Union.

Mrs. Marya Somova, assistant manager of the
Stalingrad city government, explains that the administrator looks after the needs of the tenants,
calling electricians and plumbers when necessary and hiring the ubiquitous women street-
cleaners for the area under the administrator's
jurisdiction. There is no doubt the administrators
do these things. But the Moscow resident also
observes that they have political functions, such
as telling the tenants about the local deputy up
for election.

Actually, their political activities are intensive.
Most of them are police agency people or closely
affiliated with those agencies. They are supposed
to check on the political reliability of the tenants,
reporting their comings and goings, their guests
and their habits. It may be they do less of this
now than formerly, but no one supposes they
have stopped doing it.

Beyond all this are the big control mecha-
nisms. The Communist party itself is one, with
its members strategically located in every possible organization and enterprise. To keep tabs
on teen-agers and people in their early twenties
are the Komsomol (Communist Youth) organi-

zations; for kids there are the Young Pioneers. There are still plenty of plain-clothes security men about. The MVD still has its own armed troops, an army of undetermined size, in case things ever got rough.

And whatever the current amelioration of the police state atmosphere, the atmosphere of the state itself is everywhere, oppressive and vast. Whether he buys a pack of cigarets or a bottle of beer, gets a haircut, reads a book or goes to the movies, the Soviet citizen is blanketed by the state. There is almost nothing he can do and nowhere he can go that the state is not at his side. For the most part he can learn only what the state chooses to tell him.

Still, depressing as it is, the atmosphere is unquestionably better than it was three, four and five years ago. The terror has been removed at least from the surface of life.

But as the people of Hungary know, if it is ever decided to send the terror walking the streets again, the machines for unloosing it are ready and waiting.

4...

Volga Voyage

WHILE A CANAL IN EGYPT was disturbing the peace, a canal here in Russia was disturbing the tempers of a small band of travelers. But in this case the cause was not stormy political weather; just stormy weather.

The river steamer normally takes a little over 48 hours to cover the 390 miles from Stalingrad to Rostov-on-Don via the Volga-Don Canal. This time the trip took 94 hours, or about as long as it takes some ships to cross the Atlantic.

Only a handful of first-class passengers boarded the "Mayakovsky" in Stalingrad that Saturday afternoon, and in all three classes there were only about 150 passengers on a ship with a capacity of 355, according to Captain Ivan Dobrov. Built in Hungary in 1952, with a beautiful engine made in Kiev, U.S.S.R., the "Mayakovsky" seemed a pleasant little ship on first inspection, though familiarity was to breed dislike.

The side-wheeler put out into the broad muddy Volga only 45 minutes behind schedule and steamed uneventfully into the dusk, her red flag flapping in the breeze. Not quite 19 miles southwest of Stalingrad we approached the entrance of the Volga-Don Canal, the Soviet Union's newest and biggest, begun in late 1948 and completed only four years ago. At the Volga entrance is one of those tiresome examples of Soviet art — a mammoth statue of Stalin; the figure alone is some 66 feet high and including the base it goes up 150 feet.

The ship turned west into the Canal and almost immediately was closed in the first of the nine ascending locks; each rises an average of 39 feet and each works automatically, with only one person in attendance. We were still going through these and the first four of the descending locks after dinner and through the night.

The next morning after breakfast — there were no eggs on board, so one traveler's breakfast consisted daily of hard cheese, bread, mineral water and weak coffee — most of the first-class passengers were in the tiny lounge at the "Mayakovsky's" prow.

An ancient Armenian with big white mustaches was vigorously playing the harmonica. An Argentine writer, who was traveling with his wife and

teen-age boy and little girl, was conversing with
his interpreter. The others included a big hearty
Red Army lieutenant-colonel with two silver
front teeth and a pleasant looking Russian civilian on six-months' leave from his job as engineer
in the Siberian gold-fields.

The lieutenant-colonel and the engineer af-
fected the costume so popular at Russian resorts,
which looks like pajamas and is so called in
Russian, though actually it is a form of sports-
wear. Of the two, the officer's garb looked more
like ordinary pajamas, a two-piece job of striped
green silky seeming material. The civilian's was
dressier. He wore dark solid green trousers, and
over his shirt and tie the pajama-type jacket — in
green stripes — was similar to a smoking jacket.

By this time we were beyond the thirteenth
lock and in the approach to the Zimulanskaya Sea
(actually a big lake), which separates the thirteenth from the fourteenth and fifteenth locks of
the Canal. The Zimulanskaya is 112 miles long
and, at its maximum, nearly 19 miles wide.

Then — that is, about 10 o'clock on Sunday
morning — the first blow fell. We were, we
learned, tying up at a landing station and would
be there till seven that evening, because of a big
storm in the Zimulanskaya; high above sea level
on an open steppe, it gets terrific winds.

Still, the delay seemed then no great inconvenience. The day was raw and rainy with a bitter wind but at the mooring station the ship was steady and the day passed agreeably enough. The lounge was cozy and the food (apart from breakfast) reasonably good.

Seven p. m. came, however, and there was no let-up in the weather. We would not be able to leave before morning, and it was far from certain we could leave then. Could we abandon ship and proceed by rail? No. The landing station was called "Five Houses" and that's about what it consisted of. There was no railway anywhere near, and we were not allowed to get off the ship even to look around. We were stuck in the middle of nowhere; more accurately, about 340 miles from Rostov and no other way to get there.

From this point things began to get downright disagreeable. The wind rose higher. Even at our mooring station the ship was now bobbing like the proverbial cork. The not-unattractive cabin, about five feet by ten, with a tiny desk and wash-basin, seemed more cramped than the night before. The bed seemed harder, the blanket shorter and thinner, the radio in the next cabin noisier. And it was cold, even with an overcoat thrown over the blanket.

Throughout the night loud gusts of wind tossed

the ship. The shutter at the window beat a steady
tattoo. The cabin door, though closed tight,
creaked continuously like something out of Edgar
Allan Poe.

The next morning still brought no news as to
when we might get going. There was no heat all
day (there never had been any hot water on the
ship) and in the first-class quarters it was so
cold you could see your breath. The tarpaulin
put up to protect the front windows of the lounge
banged furiously in the wind. Inside the lounge
four passengers played dominoes, looking for all
the world like four Russians playing dominoes in
a Russian ship. All afternoon there was no electricity.

Though some travelers were growing increasingly restive, the third-class passengers were taking things passively enough. They even had some
entertainment on occasion, when a sailor would
bring out his accordion. The sailors danced sometimes with each other and sometimes with waitresses or girls from the third-class quarters. But
the high point was a solo performance, a sailor
doing the "Yabluchko," or "Small Apple," on the
iron floor below decks. It is one of those violent,
arms-folded, squatting, leg-kicking dances for
which the Russians are famous.

Toward evening on Monday it grew calm

where the "Mayakovsky" was moored, but the
word was that out in the Zimulanskaya itself the
big blow was still on. On that cheerless note we
prepared to spend a second night at "Five Houses" and our third night out from Stalingrad. A
little after 10, however, a good deal of scurry-
ing could be heard on the landing station and it
became evident that we were shoving off at last.
It was a wonderful feeling.

With the coming of daylight one could see why
the authorities had refused to entrust the flat-
bottomed "Mayakovsky" to the mercies of a
stormy Zimulanskaya. For stretches no land was
visible in any direction; much of the time one
could at most discern what seemed to be the faint
outline of shore far to the south. We had been
crossing that lake ever since we left "Five
Houses" the night before and we continued to
cross it all day Tuesday. It was slow going, add-
ing to the time already lost at the landing station.

For though the worst of the storm had passed,
the lake was still rough, and it never did get
calm the whole time we were on it. The "Mayakovsky" both pitched and rolled, to the tune of
tinkling glasses in the dining room.

White-capped waves of respectable height
vigorously washed the windows of our topmost

deck. Again came the question of how long we could keep going, and when we pulled into another landing station it looked as though we were stuck once more. But it turned out to be a routine stop and we moved on.

After nightfall Tuesday — the fourth night out from Stalingrad — we finally went down through the fourteenth and fifteenth locks of the Canal and thereafter turned south into the gentle Don River. Morning showed shorescapes of a most inviting aspect; fields, but more often thick forests or spacious woods, with ashtrees at the riverbanks yellowing in the autumn sun, and in the distance, set back from the river, the bluffs of the Don Basin. It all had an untenanted, almost primeval look; for a long time there was no town and not a single Soviet monument, emblem or sign.

This, of course, is the home ground of the Don Kazaks (Cossacks), originally Russian serfs who escaped their masters to settle here. About two hours before Rostov you see in the distance the onion cupolas of the Byzantine-Russian style cathedral of Staricherkask, the ancient capital of the Don Cossacks.

And so the "Mayakovsky" came at last — uneventfully as it had started — to Rostov, just short of four full days after leaving Stalingrad. It seemed more like four weeks, and the debarking passengers, while perhaps not prepared to kiss the ground, were plenty glad to get back on it.

The moral of which, if any, is probably that it is best not to schedule a Volga-Don trip in late fall. Or perhaps that it is unwise to take anything for granted, especially in Russia.

5...

The Perils of Planning

RUSSIA'S INDUSTRY is grinding out goods at a steadily rising rate. But it still lags far behind the U. S. — a fact of major significance amid current world tensions.

According to Soviet statistics, which Western experts consider reasonably accurate, the Russians have boosted steel output from 27.3 million metric tons in 1950 to 45.3 million last year. The hope is to hike the total to 68 million by 1960. But even this goal seems small when compared with 1955 U. S. output of over 100 million metric tons.

Soviet pig iron output has jumped from 19.2 million metric tons in 1950 to 33.3 million in 1955, and by 1960 it's supposed to hit 53 million, compared with 1955 U. S. output of nearly 71 million metric tons.

In consumer goods, the contrast is even more striking. The Soviets last year turned out 151,400

40

household refrigerators, a vast increase over the 1950 figure of only 1,200 but still tiny in comparison with last year's U. S. production of nearly 4 million units. Russia in 1955 produced a shade over 4 million radios and television sets, nearly four times its 1950 output but still only about one-sixth of U. S. production.

Or consider a more prosaic item: Shoes. Alexander Chernischov, the affable director of Shoe Factory No. 4 in Kiev, the third largest Soviet city, says national shoe production now is running at an annual rate of about 350 million pairs. The 1960 goal is 455 million, or a little better than two pairs per Soviet citizen. By contrast, U. S. shoe factories last year turned out 510 million pairs — an average of about three pairs for each American.

Shoes not only come out of Soviet factories in smaller quantities but also in fewer styles. Mr. Chernischov's factory makes a full line of men's, women's and children's shoes, plain and fancy. With a total work force of 3,800, it is currently turning out about 50 different styles, but at peak demand periods of the year it may produce as many as 80.

In the U. S., a single plant may turn out even fewer styles. A typical U. S. factory concentrates on mass production of a few styles. But a U. S.

shoe company, with a number of factories, may turn out 300 to 400 styles of men's shoes, 500 or more styles of women's shoes and some 200 styles of children's footwear.

How does Mr. Chernischov decide what shoe styles to produce, in what quantity and at what prices?

The quick answer is that he doesn't decide; the state tells him, and all other factory managers regardless of product, how much to make and at what price. But that only begs the question. How does the state know?

This is the basic economic problem confronting Soviet planners. It arises because the Soviet Union does not have an economy in which, as in the United States, production, styles and prices are largely determined by the indirect bargaining of consumer and producer. Through this process, the economists will tell you, the market economy performs its most important function — the direction of resources in such a way as to permit balanced growth.

Here in the Soviet Union, by contrast, total planning is substituted for the market, in theory anyway. So the question becomes, how do the planners know what to plan, and how do they keep the economy from getting completely out of whack?

No one knows the whole answer. But one starting place is the political decision of the rulers to maintain a huge military establishment — currently being used as a prop for Hungary's puppet government and as a threat in the troubled Mid-East. In no small degree, this decision helps the planners shape the rest of the economy.

"There is politics in every plan," says N. K. Baibakov, Chairman of the State Planning Commission (Gosplan), over excellent coffee and cognac in his office in the Council of Ministers building as the snow swirls through the Moscow dusk outside.

The fact that the rulers feel it necessary, as a matter of international politics, to have a war machine equal or close to that of the U. S. enables the planners to reach one big decision — to put much more emphasis on heavy industry than on consumer goods. Out of a gross investment of 160.8 billion rubles ($40.2 billion at the artificial official exchange rate) this year, heavy industry gets 96.6 billion, light and food industries a puny 7.8 billion.

The contrast, it's true, is not quite as stark as it looks. The heavy industry figure includes allocations for housing. And investment in agriculture (21.3 billion rubles this year) also benefits the consumer. Even so, Soviet figures show that heavy industry's share of total production rose from 68.8% in 1950 to 70.6% in 1955, while the proportion devoted to consumer production fell from 31.2% to 29.4%. This means that while the volume of consumer production is increasing all the time, its relative rate of growth is nonetheless slowing.

Within this framework the planners must make rather arbitrary decisions about what things to push at what times. Until recently, for instance, housing got little attention. But the need became so urgent that they had to decree a big construction program. From 1951 through 1955, 144.2 million square meters of urban housing were put up, or roughly a fourth of the total of 640 million square meters in use at the end of last year.

But an intriguing, if not the most important, part of the answer to the question of what kinds of things to make begins to show up as you look at factories in operation and talk to planners. Within the ponderous superstructure of bureaucratic direction — there are no less than 48 Soviet ministries concerned with economics, many of them duplicated in the individual republics — a primitive kind of market economy does operate.

"For cost reasons," says Mr. Chernischov, who looks something like an enlarged version of George Gobel, complete with modified crew-cut, "we'd naturally rather keep down the number of styles, but the stores insist on new ones." The stores, in turn, are motivated by the desire to sell more, and their ideas on what kinds of styles people want come from suggestions, requests and complaints of the customers — in other words, from the market-place. In addition, the customer has his say by just not buying a particular style, thus forcing the factory to discontinue it.

The disagreement between store and factory over how many styles is resolved through meetings of representatives of each, plus officials of the government ministries concerned. At the moment it looks as though the customers, through the stores, are making their influence felt to some extent; on the average, Mr. Chernischov's plant brings out new styles twice a year, but for some women's shoes the style is changed every month.

And Mr. Chernischov tries to keep up with style trends in other countries. He is proud of what he calls his California sandals, which do in fact look like California sandals.

The "market" also plays some role in determining what things heavy industry should make. The decision that the Moscow Automobile Plant named after Likhachev (it was named after Stalin until last spring) should produce two basic

truck models, which can be subsequently modified as dump trucks, fire engines or whatever,
was not taken in a vacuum. It was the result of
surveys of needs and consultations, via the various ministries, with the end users of the trucks.

The same is true of the big Stalingrad Tractor
Plant named after Dzerzhinsky. The plant makes
two sizes of tractors. Alexander Glazov, chief
of the technical department of the tractor plant,
says entirely new models are rarely introduced,
but the existing models are constantly being
adapted and improved — to some extent in accordance with the views of the collective farms
and other customers.

"Soviet planning," says Gosplan Chairman
Baibakov, "is from the bottom up as well as from
the top down." In theory, at least, factory managers get some of their ideas about what, how
much and how to produce from the workers, and
these are incorporated into their own plans,
which are sent to the appropriate republic ministry, modified and eventually find their way to
Gosplan. Meantime, Gosplan has been devising
its own master plan, with which the local efforts
must be reconciled, often enough to the disad-
vantage of the latter.

For when it comes to the question of how
much of anything to produce, the Soviet "mar-

ket" has, in most cases, a ready answer — as much as possible. For a long time to come, Soviet officials will not have to worry about lack of demand. The problem is to produce faster and, even more fundamentally, to decide how to divide the available resources as between, say, washing machines and refrigerators.

The grass-roots planning that filters up to Gosplan cannot provide a final answer to the question of dividing up the resources pie. But, on top of the basic political decision to stress heavy industry, it helps the planners see where needs are greatest. On that basis they can decide the time has come to step up, say, refrigerator production even if it means slowing down washing machine output.

With some goods the volume of production is simply enough determined by the availability of raw materials. "We have the capacity to produce lots more shoes," says one top planner, "but we're short of leather." This partly influenced the decision as to how much to invest in agriculture — the more animals, the more leather.

How good is Russian production and the production methods behind it? It would take a host of experts to do more than generalize. Mr. Chernischov's shoes, for example, are certainly excellent by Soviet standards, but they are behind

the West's in style and — from the looks of them
— durability.

Soviet cars are definitely behind. The special-
order Zil (formerly Zis) limousine produced at
the Moscow auto factory is still essentially the
1942 Packard from which it was originally
copied. But take a spin in a tractor hot off the
Stalingrad assembly line as the driver tests
brakes, gears, steering (it turns on a dime) and
you find yourself in what seems to be an efficient,
serviceable machine, if not the most modern
looking one in the world.

At the Transcaucasian Metallurgical Combine
in Rustavi, in the Republic of Georgia, the six
open-hearth furnaces in the steel mill have doors
which open and close automatically. A complex
of about 35 shops covering an area whose per-
imeter measures about 10 miles, Transcaucasian
makes steel which it turns into its main product,
seamless pipe.

According to David Tkeshelashvili, the Georgian assistant director of the plant, it is one of
the most modern such integrated factories in
the U.S.S.R., though ranking only twelfth or
thirteenth in production. In the rolling mill, one
woman pulls levers to run a complex part of the
operation. The plant has its own institute to
speed the introduction of automation.

At Stalingrad Tractor, in one of the assembly shops, one worker operates 16 lathes; cylinder boring is also automatic. By 1960 the plant hopes to have 126 automatic lines for various parts of the assembly. But on today's assembly line, floorboards, hoods and many other parts are inserted by hand; the tractor belts are linked by a man wielding a sledge hammer.

Kiev's Shoe Factory No. 4 has plenty of machines — yet, like most other plants, what appears to be a superabundance of workers. Many of them, here and elsewhere, are women; in some plants you find them doing heavy labor. Rakhmil Lapatukhin, engineer for safety techniques at Transcaucasian's coking plant, says the proportion of women workers there is only about 10% of the 8,000 workers, not counting the additional 1,000 clerical employes. At Stalingrad Tractor, Mr. Glazov says the proportion is about 25%. At Kiev Shoe Factory No. 4 it is about 80% — but that is light industry.

Official Soviet figures show that the proportion of women in the whole work force of 48.4 million (excluding collective farm families) is 45% as against 38% in 1940. Of the 17.4 million people employed in Soviet industry, the proportion of women is also 45%, compared with 41% in 1940.

In one industry in particular the methods are
plainly pretty terrible. That is construction. As
Pavel Bopchenok, chief engineer of Leningrad's
Building Trust No. 102, shows you around a
group of partly prefabricated apartment buildings now going up in that city, you see exposed
wires running to the ceiling light in the living
room, exposed pipes and exposed radiators.

The flats in this group have private baths, but
that is by no means typical of all housing now
being built. In every Soviet city are buildings
one, two and three years old where the plaster
is flaking and the ceilings cracking. One estimate
is that maintenance and repair costs run 60%
to 80% of construction costs.

If "market" forces influence, however feebly
and indirectly, the volume and nature of Soviet
production, they also are felt in the determination
of prices; that is, the various ministries set prices
on the basis of labor and raw material costs plus
profits. But the real key is profits, for it is on its
share of these plus the stiff turnover tax slapped
on between production and distribution that the
state depends heavily for revenues. State profits
and the turnover tax add up to one very good
reason why Soviet prices are sky-high.

A Gosplan aide in Moscow says factory profits
range from 6% to 12%. Of this "planned" profit

— that is, what Gosplan thinks the factory should make — 3% to 5% is left to the factory and the rest goes to the state budget. But if the factory makes more than its planned profit, 30% to 50% of the excess stays with the plant, the rest going to the state. The factory's share of the unplanned profit can be used for various projects — including, for example, building kindergartens and nurseries or establishing a fund from which to loan workers money to build their own private homes.

It's hard to get anybody to turn these percentages into figures, though. Ivan Karzov, assistant director of the Moscow auto plant, will cheerfully reveal the sales prices of the Zil 150 truck— 13,500 rubles ($3,375). But he won't tell the cost. "That's our secret," Mr. Karzov says, adding that the plant is "very profitable."

Factory executives, at any rate, are very much interested in cost-cutting. For one thing, as Mr. Tkeshelashvili says, the state insists on progressively lower costs. Besides, there seems to be a certain amount of human pride in doing better than the other fellow. Mr. Glazov estimates, with no displeasure, that Stalingrad Tractor makes the big tractor 1,000 rubles cheaper than the same type is made in another city.

But since the state which sets the prices also

sets the costs--that is, the price of labor and raw materials—how can a factory manager cut costs? Mainly the answer is that the manager has considerable leeway about the organization of his own shop. If he can cut corners on the use of raw materials without producing an inferior end-product, he is free to do it. He can save in countless other ways—even on electricity and heat (in Mr. Chernischov's office the temperature seemed about zero).

"Economy, economy," says Mr. Chernischov happily, "we think about it constantly."

6...

The Hard Buy

"WOMEN'S DRESSES 30% OFF" proclaims a big sign in the Univermag (department store) on Stalingrad's Square of Dead Warriors. The reduced dresses are on circular racks behind a railing in one corner of the first floor.

In Moscow at the Univermag at No. 11 Novo-pechanya (New Sand) St. in the suburb of Sokol, Manager Yuri Illitch has a special counter piled with ready-made dresses, also reduced about 30%.

And at the huge GUM (State Universal Store) in Moscow's Red Square, across from the Lenin-Stalin mausoleum and the Kremlin, Assistant Manager Boris Tolstikov points to a streamer arching over one of the arcades which make up this labyrinthine building. The streamer says: "20% to 60% Off," with an arrow indicating where these bargains can be found. "Means a loss for us," remarks Mr. Tolstikov ruefully.

In short, Soviet store managers have headaches not unlike those of their counterparts elsewhere—though naturally there are also some
rather basic differences. They have to worry not
only about dealing with goods that don't sell
well, but also about such highly "capitalistic"
problems as profits and competition.

"If we've had a dress 20 months and it hasn't
sold, the price is cut," says Anna Mikhailovna,
the saleswoman behind the barrier in the Stalingrad Univermag. But can Soviet store executives
decide to cut prices on their own?

It isn't quite that simple in the Communist
economy. For one thing, the government now
orders price cuts on individual goods from time
to time, in place of the general annual price reductions that used to prevail. Apart from that,
a particular store must go through the Ministry
of Trade before it can put a lower price tag on
an item.

Thus when Mr. Tolstikov, a pleasant bald
gentleman who started working in the retail
business in pre-revolutionary times at the age
of 11, finds a lemon on his hands he tells the
Ministry and the Ministry sends a representative
around to find out why the article isn't selling.
Then the Ministry and GUM come to an agree-
ment on how much to cut the price.

But if the Ministry decides the item is really terrible in quality or appearance, it will confer with the appropriate production ministry, and in due course output will be halted. This happened to one model refrigerator, the predecessor of the current "North 2" made by the Moscow Gas Works. People just didn't buy the original model because it wasn't decorative enough, Mr. Tolstikov says. So the plant put the old machine in a new and prettier box; it's now selling all right.

How does a Communist store get its "profits"? At the moment, for one example, Mr. Tolstikov has 10 "Dneper" model tape recorders in stock in the appliance section. Before he ordered them, he and the factory knew—because the Ministry of Trade sets almost all retail prices—that they would retail at 1,500 rubles ($375 at the artificial official exchange rate) each or 15,000 for the lot. Of this 15,000, GUM keeps 5%, or 750, and the rest goes to the factory. Different items carry different percentages; the average is about 6½%.

"That's our bonus," beams Mr. Tolstikov. Out of it must come wages and maintenance and a percentage for the state as well as operating reserves for the store. Not surprisingly the "bonus" is a matter of keen interest to store managers.

The real incentive, though, is the "norm,"

which in the case of stores is the sales volume
that must be met or exceeded; it differs from
store to store, based on the past performance of
each. For Mr. Illitch's emporium in Sokol, this
year's norm is five million rubles (over $1.2 mil-
lion) a month; last year, it was over four million
a month, the year before 3.5 million. By contrast
GUM — which has 5,500 employes and on an
average day greets 250,000 visitors and wraps
160,000 parcels—sells 10 million rubles' worth of
goods a day.

The steady boosting of norms is naturally calculated to keep a manager on his toes. And despite that fact that the same item sells at the
same price everywhere in the Soviet Union except at some far distant points, it means that
there is a certain amount of competition; in order
to fulfill his own norm, the store manager has to
be alert to what others are doing. Store managers
usually don't call it competition, or at most call
it "peaceful" or "social" competition, but it shows
up in such ways as better service in one store or
more attentive salespeople in another.

In Mr. Illitch's neighborhood, for instance, is
a special TV and radio shop. Yet Mr. Illitch, a
short, slight, rather intense man in his forties,
says that when he opened his own TV and radio
department people began coming to him be-

cause he makes a point of very carefully checking the sets first and thereafter of providing very
good service.

Or listen to a saleslady at the Shop of Presents,
opened less than a year ago on Moscow's Gorki
St. Why, she is asked, does a customer buy a
2,500-ruble ($625) set of china at this store
when he can buy the same thing at the same
price at GUM and other stores? Her reply is that
the Shop of Presents is a particularly beautiful
place (it is in fact quite attractive), isn't as
crowded as a vast maze like GUM and puts considerable stress on pleasing the customer.

Stores do differ strikingly from each other,
which seems to indicate—to some extent, at least
—the managers' differing ideas of how to compete for the sales ruble. Naturally, the main
Stalingrad Univermag is not as big and handsome as GUM. Stalingrad has only 525,000
people, compared with Moscow's nearly five
million, and Moscow is the capital of the country.

But consider Tiflis, capital of Georgia. On one
side of Lenin Square in the center of the city is
one Univermag. It's dirty, dimly lighted, with
sawdust on the floor and goods heaped every
which way on counters. It reminds you of a picture of a general store out of the last century.

Right across the square is another store, also

called a Univermag but chiefly selling a full line
of men's and women's clothes. Here suits, dresses
and hats are given special displays, often on
dummies, and the whole place is much cleaner
and more spacious than the other store.

The competitive spirit induced by norms gets
right down to the individual employe. The average GUM worker makes a minimum of 700
rubles ($175) a month, but can get up to 900 or
even more by exceeding his norm. In some cases,
this works in reverse as well.

For example, Antonina Giorgievna, bookkeeper
of a Gastronom (state grocery) in Sokol, explains thaat an average employe's norm there is
4,700 rubles of sales a month; on this basis his
salary is 462 rubles (about $115) a month. But
if he fails to meet the norm he gets only 90% of
that sum. So it behooves him to "compete" with
the other clerks.

All the same, a visitor is not struck by the
aggressiveness of the salesmanship in the Soviet
Union. Since there is too little of almost everything, it is more often the customers who seem
aggressive.

If the Soviet store manager shares some of
the problems of his retailers elsewhere, he is
nonetheless free—if that is the word—of other
worries. Most obviously, perhaps, no executive

here is an owner, and so has no money of his own at stake in the enterprise.

Then, too, the Russian retailer doesn't have to bother his head much about advertising. When the Shop of Presents opened, the state radio announced the fact, describing what kind of store it was and where, and that was pretty much that. Occasionally an ad for a store will appear in the "Evening Moscow" newspaper, and sometimes a store will get the radio to announce some special offering. But most advertising is by word of mouth.

In fact, the store manager doesn't even have to supply a distinctive name for his establishment. The name of a dress shop is "Store for Women's Clothing." A barbershop is "Barbershop No. 9" or whatever. Mr. Illitch's store is just one of a flock of Moscow Univermags—there are seven others in Sokol alone—but people know it is the one on Novopechanya St. A Gastronom is a Gastronom, often in neon lights.

In a store such as GUM and in other big stores in big cities like Leningrad and Kiev, considerable attention is paid to attractive display, though there is no evidence of any attempt to promote one product against another. But the average store manager doesn't seem to worry much about appearances, or sometimes even whether the goods he wants to sell are clearly visible at all.

What's it like shopping in these places? If an American had to do it as a regular thing, it would probably drive him crazy in short order.

First of all, prices are steep, even though they are not as high as they were several years ago. Goods are expensive when translated into dollars, but more significantly they are expensive when translated into Soviet incomes. Some non-Soviet sources reckon the national average income at 600 to 650 rubles ($150.00-$162.50) a month. Since most wives work, the average family income might be somewhere in the neighborhood of 1,000 rubles ($250) a month.

With that in mind, consider these random prices: The cheapest TV set in Mr. Illitch's establishment, equipped with a microscopic screen, is 850 rubles. The best, with only a slightly larger screen, costs 2,000—two months' income. An ordinary bike will run 650-750.

In the window of a Moscow men's store is a typical Russian-style suit—bell-bottom trousers and fingertip jacket sleeves—selling for 1,660, or over six weeks' income. In the Stalingrad store, salesgirl Valentina Grigorievna will show you suits from 400 rubles to 1,755. In the Tiflis clothing store there is one for 1,805, but in the junkier department store across from it the range is from 440 to 879.

The reduced price on a crepe de chine dress in the Stalingrad store is 375 rubles ($93.75). In Tiflis there are ready made dresses from 336 to 709 and black dress shoes at 446 ($111.50). One pair of men's brown oxfords in Stalingrad sells for 292, another for 346.

At GUM a vacuum cleaner with seven attachments resembling the original Lewyt model costs 650 rubles. The smallest refrigerator costs 680. You can buy an unappealing, three-piece living room suite in Tiflis for 1,879 and in Stalingrad a bedroom suite for 9,930 ($2,482.50). The latter consists of twin beds, two night tables, a dresser, two chairs and a hassock.

There's no instalment buying; everything is for cash. According to Soviet Minister of Trade D. V. Pavlov, however, instalment buying will be introduced "soon," perhaps next year, on big items like furniture.

Meantime, people do buy, despite high prices and low average incomes. Raisa Marochkova, a salesgirl in the main Stalingrad Univermag, says the store sold 13 dining room suites in the last month and a half—at 7,439 rubles each.

Soviet figures on total turnover aren't too helpful because they include cooperatives and

restaurants, but for what they are worth they
show that the country's retail commodity turnover rose from 359.6 billion rubles (almost $90
billion) in 1950 to 501.5 billion rubles (over
$125 billion) in 1955. Also, the number of retail
establishments (again including public dining)
increased in the same period from 298,000 stores
and 117,000 tents to 352,400 stores and 135,100
tents.

Besides price, what might also annoy an
American suddenly transformed into a Russian is
the question of quality. Some fabrics seem excellent, but most things don't. The best men's suit
in the Stalingrad store (1,755 rubles) was described as of Polish tricot, but it is a little hard
and gritty to the touch. Also on display is an
old-fashioned metal bed for 413 rubles and old-
fashioned lampshades at 98 to 199 rubles. Most
appliances have, at best, a faintly tinny look.

In addition, the selection of brands of appliances available to the customer is modest. The
Russian's choice of refrigerators is limited to four
sizes, though there are a number of different
names, depending on where the refrigerator is
produced.

Of course, you may very well not be able to
buy what you want at all. In the Tiflis department store there is only one medium-sized re-

frigerator on display. The appliance section in this store contains mostly washtubs and pails.

Then there is the inconvenience of shopping. You will find one Gastronom for preserves, another for milk and milk products. If they do happen to be under one roof, they will be compartmentalized so that you have to go out on the street to get from one part to another. There is nothing resembling a supermarket in this country, though some self-service stores have been started.

Or take a look at a "Store for Women's Clothing" on Moscow's Gorki St. Inside, it's a long rectangle with a barrier running the width of the store. The ready-made dresses, on circular racks and on tables, are on one side of the barrier; the customers on the other. Women crowd up against the barrier two or three deep in this narrow space.

The customer points to one of the dresses she likes, and then is admitted behind the barrier so she can try it on in one of the tiny booths along the wall. If she is going to take the dress, she leaves it behind the barrier, gets a chit which she presents to the cashier outside the barrier, pays, gets her receipt, returns to the barrier and collects her dress. If she likes a dress but it isn't the right size, she can't order the right size.

However, this clumsy system may be slowly on the wane. At least Mr. Tolstikov says GUM is getting rid of the barriers as fast as it can—as a result, interestingly enough, of criticism by Americans visiting the store. In place of the barrier system, the customer in a number of GUM departments can now inspect the goods right on the counter or floor and pay for what he takes right there.

And Soviet customers can get delivery service, at least on big items and at a big store like GUM, which uses trucks from stations maintained by the Ministry of Trade and charges a small extra fee. Also, Mr. Tolstikov says, they can exchange defective items or get their money back, usually during a period of five days but up to six months on durables like refrigerators.

7...

Portrait of Olga

OLGA V. was born in Moscow in 1933, in the sixteenth year of Soviet power in Russia. She has never traveled outside the Soviet Union, and very little within it. She is at least fairly typical of educated Soviet young people.

What goes on in Olga's mind, and what educational forces formed that mind?

A rather plain girl who could be much prettier if she would use lipstick and could dress better, Olga not surprisingly views life, the world and herself through red-colored glasses. What is surprising is that her views are not more fanatic and dogmatic than they are—that, considering her background, there are any small windows at all in her closed mind.

For Olga indoctrination in Communism, or Marxism-Leninism as it is more commonly called here, began with her three R's, in the autumn of 1942. Most children now begin the first grade in elementary school at the age of seven. But Olga was a year late because the German attack had disrupted the school system in 1941.

The subjects in the early grades are about the same as anywhere else—except for the basic difference that literally everything is taught from the beginning in the perspective of Marxism-Leninism. From the first grade Olga knew there were two types of political theories, Capitalism and Communism, and she knew which one was bad and which good.

In the third grade, Olga joined the Young Pioneers. "It would be hard to find a child who does not join," she explains. This organization covers the age range from 10 to 14. The members have a local Palace of Young Pioneers in which they spend—or at least Olga spent—about six hours a week after school. The kids join one or more "circles," meaning groups devoted to dancing, singing, sewing, aviation models and the like.

Normally the Young Pioneers don't wear a uniform, though they get a distinguishing red tie and button, but for ceremonial occasions they have a "camp" uniform consisting in the case of girls of a dark skirt, white shirt and red tie. The Moscow Young Pioneers may take part in the big parades on May Day, November 7 (anniversary of the revolution) and other holidays. In summer they go to Young Pioneer camps in the country.

How much indoctrination comes through this door? Olga would have you believe not much, but from other sources it is clear there is plenty. In fact, the Young Pioneers is not only an indoctrination device but also one part of the Communist control apparatus for checking on political reliability — yes, even of youngsters.

Olga does concede that twice a month or so the YP's get special lectures in their palaces, about world conditions and books and so forth. In any case, Olga says, throughout the 10 grades of elementary school it's Marxism-Leninism day in and day out in the classroom. There's no special course in the subject at this level; it's simply the basis of all courses.

Along about the fourth grade, though, special emphasis begins to be placed on politics, especially in connection with ancient history, and by the seventh grade the children are learning in some detail about the political "contributions" of the U.S.S.R.

Concurrent with this continuing political education is the teaching of atheism. Again, there is no special course in atheism; the children are simply taught, through such courses as ancient

history and geography, that the various religions
are the result of the stupid imaginings of early
people, as Olga puts it, and that the only accept-
able basis for viewing man and the universe is
the scientific (meaning atheistic in this usage)
one.

By the ninth and tenth grades, the Marxist-
Leninist angle is getting hotter. The youngsters
are now studying a pamphlet on labor by Engels;
they are learning, in simplified form, Marxist explanations of "why economic conditions are bad
for workers in other countries."

When she was 14, in sixth grade, Olga de-
parted the Young Pioneers and joined the Komsomol (Communist Youth League). This is not
formally a branch of the Communist party, and
its members — just about everybody from 14 to
24 —do not automatically go on to join the party.
In a number of ways it carries forward, in more
advanced form, the activities of the Young
Pioneers.

But there are new activities too. For example,
when an election is coming up, say for the Su-
preme Soviet or a local people's court, the Kom-
somols trot around to apartments in their district
of the city, telling the people about the deputy
up for election in that district. Budding poli-
ticians in a one-party state. The Komsomol, of

course, is another part of the indoctrination-control mechanism.

After graduating from 10th grade, Olga applied for the Pedagogical Institute of Moscow (an institute is roughly comparable to a college in the U. S.), took the necessary exams and was admitted. As the name implies, the four-year course (it is now five) trains future teachers in the specialized subject of their choice. Again, the curriculum is not unusual, as far as the names of courses go—psychology, a modern foreign language, literature, pedagogy, history, Latin.

Here, however, begin the formal courses in Marxism-Leninism and they go on until graduation. The first year Olga had the origins of M-L, covering the French revolutionists, the 19th century Russian revolutionists, the revolutionary situation in Russia at the end of the 19th century and the first (1905) Russian revolution.

At the same time the students are studying the actual works of Marx and Engels, with particular emphasis on "Das Kapital" the first two years. Olga had to write a theme about once a week; a typical subject might be "Why Communism Came to Exist," based on the Communist Manifesto and other works. These M-L classes met twice a week the first year, later once a week.

In the third year the Marxism-Leninism course
is called Political Economy and treats the economy of the capitalist countries. Not, however,
country by country but in general, with examples
drawn from individual nations—and more from
Britain than from the U. S. The fourth year M-L
course, Dialectical Materialism, is chiefly concerned with the economy of the Soviet Union,
Communist China and the "people's democra-
cies" of Eastern Europe.

Olga was graduated from the Institute and
plans to teach, though she has not yet sought a
post—perhaps next year, when she will also be
getting married. She is still a Komsomol, but does
not now participate in any of its activities.

She has not decided whether to apply for
membership in the Communist party, but this
implies no disrespect; on the contrary, she calls
it the "first front" in the people's interests, and
not all 200 million Soviet citizens can be in the
first front. Actually only about seven million are
party members.

Despite her indigestible scholastic diet, Olga
seems a perfectly normal person in non-political
matters; certainly she does not resemble the
stereotype of the grim "Soviet woman." She has
a pleasant, friendly personality and a sense of
humor. And for all the Communism plus atheism,

it would be hard to demonstrate that her moral values are inferior to those in Western countries; they seem about the same.

Concerning matters of Communist and international politics, though, her thinking—inevitably it would seem—parrots what she has learned in school and what she now reads in the Soviet papers and magazines and hears on the Soviet radio.

To Olga, for instance, the Suez dispute is very simple: The U. S. is against Egypt's rights. However, she wants her interlocutor to explain the American view. Did North Korea attack South Korea or vice versa in June, 1950? Olga doesn't know, but she does know that the North Koreans were in the right.

On the question of German unity she is completely foggy; she doesn't grasp that the issue turns on free elections (which the Soviets have always refused to permit). As for war, she thinks the American people don't want one, but is not sure about the American government and claims no opinion as to whether war is likely or less or more likely than a few years ago.

This haze on foreign affairs in a well-educated person is a signal tribute to the startling lack of foreign news in the Soviet press and the distorted form it takes when it appears. During the

New York negotiations Suez got a fairly big play on the back page, but that was about all the news of the outside world.

Olga also sounds confused about the United States economy, but that is perhaps a better sign than if she were dogmatically certain about it. At one point when asked what she thought conditions were like in the U. S., she said, "I think they are as described by Theodore Dreiser." But she quickly countered: "Is that in fact correct?" And she asked many, many questions about all aspects of American life.

At another point she said she thought the workers in the U. S. were pretty well off and had been for some time, because America is the richest of the capitalist nations and did not suffer destruction in the war. This admission of a certain amount of well-being in the U. S. reflects the current Soviet government line, which is to admit a temporary prosperity but to explain it in snide terms. Olga said she thought there is unemployment in the U. S., however, but not as much as in Britain and other Western countries.

She is dogmatic when she tells you that capitalism is dying, though. How does she know? Because history teaches that such is the way with politico-economic forms; capitalism will be replaced by socialism, which will be replaced by

Communism which won't be replaced by anything because it will be utopia. So you get a little
dose of historical materialism, gratis. Still, Olga
is far from sure that the death of capitalism will
occur any time soon; "who knows what will happen in the next hundred or two hundred years?"

Was she startled by the Soviet government
campaign of vilification launched against the late
Stalin earlier this year? Yes, rather; but she
thought it "high time" and believes the party is
quite right to criticize him. All the same she
thinks his contributions are very important despite his many mistakes. Have the present leaders done more for the people since the war than
Stalin did? Yes, she thinks so. What sort of man
is Communist party secretary Khrushchev? She
considers, then: "I think he is a very clever man."

In all this it is possible to read considerable
doubt and hesitation which, for all one knows,
may represent an intellectual upheaval in the
minds of Olga and those like her. Certainly it
is tempting to think what a couple of years in
the West might do to open this mind.

But it would be unwise to infer too much.
There are all those years of undiluted Marxism-
Leninism, not to mention the constant propaganda bombardment every Soviet citizen gets,
and they have had their effect. You should hear

Olga stand the Anglo-Saxon concepts of political liberty on their head as she explains Soviet politics.

In such spheres talking to Olga is like trying to communicate not so much with a Marxian as with a Martian.

8...

Mr. Meged Builds His Dream House

IN THE VILLAGE of Bucha, near Kiev, Grigory
Meged is having his own home built. And in
Stalingrad, Alexei Dmitrievitch brings carrots—
via Volga boat—from his home 19 miles away
to sell at free prices in the open air market.

Private housing and free commodity markets
are the outstanding examples of growing non-
state enterprise in the Soviet Union. They are
not the only ones. Many a carpenter, electrician
and dentist makes extra money doing private
work on his own time. Some people rent out a
room or a corner of a room. In addition, there
is a good deal of illegal enterprise in the form
of black markets. And despite Communism, most
people show a strongly developed taste for private ownership; a man lucky enough to own a
small Pobeda car thinks of the day he may be
able to acquire a Zim or even a Zil.

All this does not, of course, prove that the

Soviet system is changing in the direction of private enterprise. In some ways state control is, if anything, widening. Collective farms are theoretically cooperative, non-state undertakings, but they have always been under the thumb of Moscow and still are. Producer artels, which in theory are industrial cooperatives, are rapidly being taken over by the state.

What the existence of non-state enterprise—particularly private home-building and free market farm sales—does show, in the opinion of experts on this country, is that the Soviets are perfectly willing to depart from Communist principles when they feel they have to. Some experts contend that the system wouldn't work at all on a purely Communist basis.

Need, at any rate, is the explanation for the big surge of private home building. The housing shortage is so desperate that the government, besides greatly stepping up public housing construction, is encouraging people to do it themselves.

From 1951 through 1955, 144.2 million square meters of urban housing were put up, of which 38.8 million, or more than one-fourth, were private homes. In this country, where quarters are crowded, that 144.2 million square meters is enough to accommodate an estimated 16 million people, or 4 million families of four. At the end of last year a total of 640 million square meters of urban housing were in use, of which 208 million were private. Moreover, the private trend is on the rise. In 1950, 6.4 million square meters of private homes were built; in 1955, 8.4 million.

Drive around some of the hilly outlying parts of Kiev, like the Pechersky and Stalinka regions, and you see lots of brick houses, some of them two-story, going up. (There are also many old log and clay whitewashed structures.) Stop at one of the houses a-building and you find a modest dwelling that will consist of four rooms plus kitchen, bath and veranda.

How do Soviet citizens go about buying or building, what does it cost, and where do they get the money?

It's not too difficult, as Mr. Meged, who is the manager of one section of the Kiev State Swine Farm in Bucha, will tell you. He and his wife (they have a married daughter in Odessa and a younger daughter studying in Kiev), now live in half of a two-unit house built by the farm administration in 1953.

Their present home consists of a small combination living-dining room (a tiny-screen TV set perches proudly on a table), a small bedroom and a kitchen with stove but no refrigerator. No bathroom; there is a communal bath down near the fodder kitchen. You enter the house through a small outside portico directly into the kitchen.

The house Mr. Meged is having built will be small, too, and inexpensive — only about 10,000 rubles ($2,500). Construction began last spring and Mr. Meged expects it to be finished by the end of this year. Most private homes take longer — 18 months to two years.

The 10,000-ruble cost is somewhat deceptive. It doesn't include Mr. Meged's own labor, and down on the state farm they use cheap materials. Also, Mr. Meged doesn't have to pay the workers he hires as much as city folk would; in Leningrad a skilled worker like an electrician will get one and a half to two times his normal pay for outside work on his own time. However, there is a good deal of skill-swapping; if you are a carpenter you help a plumber on his house and he helps on yours.

For this reason it's hard to estimate the cost of an average private home. In Kiev the figure is said to be about 25,000 rubles ($6,250), but in Rostov-on-Don and Tiflis you hear higher estimates, 40,000 rubles ($10,000) or more; in Moscow 35,000 rubles ($8,750) is said to be tops for an average home.

Mr. Meged is putting up 5,000 rubles of his own savings. The other 5,000 is a loan from the farm administration, to be repaid in seven years through pay deductions (unlike collective farms, state farms pay straight wages as in industry). There is no interest. In the same way a factory worker can get an interest-free loan from the factory administration or trade union or both together. Banks will also provide money to individuals, usually seven-year loans of about 10,000 rubles at 3% interest.

Though all land belongs to the state, a home builder is allotted a small plot of ground. In Kiev no rent is charged, but elsewhere, as in Rostov-on-Don, there is a nominal rent of about 100 rubles a year, paid to the local branch of the Gosbank (State Bank).

The buying and selling market, however, is not exactly brisk; when a family builds, it is likely to stay put. But when a house is sold, the buyer and seller agree on a price and go to a lawyer to close the deal, much as in other countries.

Sometimes people have to move whether they want to or not. Right after the war in Stalingrad, which was almost wiped out, people put up little whitewashed log houses; they look no bigger than children's playhouses. Now the city wants to tear

them down and put the people in apartments
that are being built or planned.

"But many don't want to move," says Mrs.
Marya Somova, assistant manager of the Stalingrad city government. The people are supposed
to get compensation, so they could presumably
build elsewhere if they don't care to go into a
flat.

Even with all this public and private building,
there is no sign of an end to the housing shortage.
A Leningrad building engineer figures it will be
10 to 15 years before housing catches up with
needs, and that is probably a highly optimistic
estimate.

The same reason — need — explains why Alexei
Dmitrievitch and his family, and the nearly 20
million other families on some 86,000 collective
farms throughout the Soviet Union, can sell their
privately-grown produce at their own prices.

The U.S.S.R. has just brought in a record grain
harvest, now estimated at somewhere around 125
million metric tons, as compared with 100 million
to 110 million last year. But there is no certainty
that agriculture, which has always been the worst
laggard of the Soviet economy, has finally turned
the corner.

Many experts doubt, for example, that the new
lands in Kazakhstan and Siberia will bring in as

good harvests every year as they did this year.
So the Soviets need not only the peasant's private
production, but perhaps even more the psycho-
logical incentive this gives him to work harder.

In the Stalingrad free market you see stall after
stall with a profusion of potatoes, pears, onions,
carrots, red peppers, radishes, eggs, chickens and
mutton—all at higher prices than charged in the
state stores where no such abundance prevails.
There is Ivan Valentinevitch, who has traveled
from Saratov 370 miles away because the Stalingrad price is better. Here selling radishes is Ma-
trena Dmietrievna, who lives only about a mile
out of Stalingrad.

In Tiflis, the capital of the Georgian Republic,
the market is in a big building, on two floors,
and the abundance is even greater. It's a real
bazaar atmosphere, with the peasants hawking
their wares and the buyers busily bargaining.

To get an idea of how this private agricultural
economy works, visit the Red Partisan Collective
Farm of the Leningrad District, just outside the
city limits. On its 2,200 hectares (nearly 5,500
acres) are 400 farm workers, including members
of families 16 and older. The main products are
milk, swine, potatoes and vegetables. Some 30
Red Partisan families, incidentally, are currently
building their own homes.

Each family has its own allotment of about one-fourth of a hectare, on which many grow strawberries, apples, pears and radishes. Strawberries are the most profitable; Pavel Saveliev says he made about 25,000 rubles ($6,250) on strawberries last year. On the other hand, Adam Stern, who has been here only a couple of years, isn't selling much of anything.

Mikhail Petrunin, manager of the Red Partisan, estimates the average income from an allotment at 15,000 to 20,000 rubles a year. Even if this estimate is considerably on the high side, a family wouldn't have to make much to overshadow its share of the collective produce sales: it's less than 6,000 rubles a year on the average, though the peasants also get various amounts of food from the farm.

On his private allotment the farmer is permitted to have one cow and two calves, no horse and an unlimited quantity of poultry and bees.

In theory the collective farm is itself a form of cooperative enterprise, with the farmers banding together to organize it and electing their manager and deciding all their problems in pure-democratic fashion. In theory the Red Partisan farmers jointly own everything you see as you trudge through the mud in a pouring rain — the clean, new (1955) swine and cattle barns (electric milkers), the poultry house with its 2,000 White Russian (Leghorn-based) hens and roosters, the 6,000 hogs, the 264 cows (most of them Black Swedish, relatives of Holstein), the 86 horses (the pride of Red Partisan is Pearl, a huge Ardennes) and all the things grown collectively. (This is one of the better collectives; at the end of 1954 only 41% of collectives had electric power.)

Actually, Stalin dragooned the peasants, with considerable trouble, into the collectives in the late Twenties and early Thirties. They are operated by and for the state and if the farmers "own" them there is little to remind them of the fact. Still, some vestiges of cooperative enterprise do remain.

Thus Mr. Petrunin estimates the farm's gross income this year at 3.5 million rubles ($875,000). Fifteen percent of that goes for capital investment and repayment of the 10-year 3% loan given by Gosbank when the farm was reorganized (it was first founded in 1930) after being razed during the war. Another 15% goes to the state as taxes. The remaining 70% covers current needs and what is left of it is distributed among the farmers at the end of the year. So there is some attempt to retain the idea of profit-sharing.

Also, the farm sells some of its collectively
produced commodities — like milk, vegetables
and potatoes — in the same free markets where
the farmers sell their private produce; the farm
can sell in this way only any excess over what it
must deliver to the state. The prices are free,
set by the manager in accordance with supply
and demand. In 1955 the private sales of individuals and collectives accounted for a little over
15% of the total sale of food commodities.

Collectives are sometimes called agricultural
artels in this country, but the industrial artel is
on the way out, as you can see by calling at No.
6 Promishlenniy Pereulok in Leningrad. Here
Mrs. Vera Bespalova presides over the Leningrad
Cooperative Textile Artel, or Lencooptextile for
short.

Theoretically, industrial artels, like collective
farms, are cooperative ventures in which artisans,
often in the handicrafts, band together, pooling
their resources and sharing the profits. In the
first years of Soviet power, some were in fact
organized that way, Mrs. Bespalova says. But
year by year they came to be organized more
and more by local soviets, or city councils. Now
the workers have the same wage scales as in state
factories, and there is little if anything of a
cooperative nature.

Yet there are some differences. The workers are supposed to elect the management. Artel workers have no trade union and no union dues. When a worker joins the artel he pays a fee of 15 rubles, and thereafter a certain part of his salary — about two and a half months' pay a year on the average — into a special artel fund.

Mrs. Bespalova, who has been with Lencoop-textile 12 years, now has 3,100 rubles ($775) in this fund. But it can hardly be called a profit-sharing arrangement. The money is simply her own, and she will get it back when she leaves or the state takes over (the state keeps the initial 15 rubles). The fund's only use seems to be as a contingency reserve in the case of fire or other accident.

In 1954 there were 114,000 industrial artels accounting for less than 6% of the gross national product; 212,000 state industrial enterprises accounted for nearly 92%. Last year between 1.6 million and 1.8 million people worked in artels, out of a total of 17.4 million workers in Soviet industry. Now the state is taking over the artels rapidly. In the third quarter of this year 42 artels of all types in Leningrad alone became state factories, according to Mrs. Bespalova.

Artels normally get the short end of the raw material and equipment stick. When a state factory gets new equipment it sends the old to an artel. In the case of Mrs. Bespalova's textile artel, it makes blankets, among other things, from cotton waste. In fact, Mrs. Bespalova indicates that this artel's main reason for existence is to use up industry waste.

Lencooptextile is going the way of the other artels; it will become a state factory in another year or two. Some artels, however, will probably continue to exist, particularly to employ handicapped persons and to serve distant, little-industrialized parts of the country.

Do the workers of Lencooptextile feel any sentimental regrets at the doom of the artel? Not at all. Mrs. Bespalova speaks of artels rather contemptuously as a rudimentary form of the organization of labor. Besides, she says, when the state takes over there may be better equipment and materials.

And Mrs. Marya Mukinya, who is a helper checking on quality, says she plans to stay on after the state takes over. She has been with the artel 25 years but has only 530 rubles in the fund (the ruble was worth more in the old days). "It's all the same to me," she explains. "I get my money back. And I have to work anyway."

9...

Buttons from Records

"THERE IS NO INFLATION in the Soviet Union," says banker Ivan Skabelkin calmly, coldly and flatly. "There can't be."

What Mr. Skabelkin, a section manager of the Gosbank (State Bank) in Moscow, means is that the government budget regularly runs a surplus. In addition, official prices have declined rather than risen over the post-war years. And observers agree that a real runaway inflation leading to economic collapse is difficult to imagine in this country.

But that is about the most that students of the Soviet financial system can say for the no-inflation thesis. Despite the budget surplus and stable prices, the evidence is overwhelming that the U.S.S.R. is in a state of chronic inflation, sometimes dangerous and always economically enervating. This makes a superficially paradoxical, but hardly mysterious, inflationary situation.

88 THROUGH SOVIET WINDOWSTHROUGH SOVIET WINDOWS

What's more, the indications are that the inflation will get worse in coming months. "We face a big problem in 1957," admits N. K. Baibakov, Chairman of the Gosplan (State Planning Commission).

First, what is the evidence of inflation right now?

An American, dining late, sits at a window table in the National Hotel restaurant here, from which he can see the outlines of part of the Kremlin wall and the fantastic onion turrets of St. Basil's Cathedral. Two Russian men, somewhat the worse for vodka, sit down at the same table. In fractured Russian and garbled German a conversation of sorts takes place.

The more presentable of the two Russians declines to say what he does for a living, but it quickly becomes clear he would like to do business. First is the mention of "valuta" — foreign exchange. Then, as a sign of "druzhba" (friendship) he wants to trade his own and his companion's fountain pens for one American pen. Later he wants to swap their two watches for one American. In other words these characters know they can find buyers willing to pay plenty of rubles for articles of a quality not obtainable in Soviet stores.

Another American is approached on the street

one night. He is offered 15 rubles to the dollar
(nearly four times the artificial exchange rate of
four to one), and 17 to the dollar if he will exchange as much as $500.

Judging from the Soviet press, black market
activity—or illegal "speculation"—in goods is also
rife, though it is impossible to tell the extent or
seriousness of it. Pure woolen fabrics are said to
be one of the leading articles in the Soviet black
market. One man in a Baltic republic of the
U.S.S.R. was prosecuted for melting down
phonograph records and making them into but-
tons, which seems a singularly unrewarding enterprise.

At two recent trials speculators were convicted
of reselling Pobeda cars, next to the smallest
here, at a profit. The car officially sells at between
17,000 and 20,000 rubles ($4,250 to $5,000). The
speculators resold them respectively at 36,000
and 38,000 rubles ($9,000 and $9,500).

Another sign of the inflationary car shortage
is the report that a Muscovite can't even get on
the waiting list for the Moskvitch, the tiniest and
cheapest Soviet car; it costs 15,000 rubles ($3,-
750) officially. The authorities wouldn't let the
waiting list go over 100,000.

Or take a look at the spread between free
market food prices and Gastronom (state gro-

cery store) prices. In the Gastronoms the prices
are set by the state. In the free markets farmers
are permitted to ask their own price for the things
they grow on their small private allotments on
the collective farms; in addition, the collective itself may sell at free prices any excess over what
it must deliver to the state.

In the Tiflis, Georgia, free market fairly large
tomatoes sell for 4 rubles ($1) a kilo (2.2 lbs.)
as against 2 or 2.50 rubles in the store. Here are
some other comparisons: Free market apples, 6
rubles a kilo, store apples 3.20; free market mutton, 28 rubles a kilo, store mutton 13; free market eggs, 12 rubles for 10, store eggs 6.50 and 7
rubles for 10. In the Stalingrad free market a
small dressed chicken costs 25 rubles compared
with 18 rubles in a Stalingrad store.

Even more indicative than the spread is the
fact many commodities available in the free market don't appear at all in the stores. The Tiflis
market offers black figs, fresh beans, parsley; a
check at the stores on the same day reveals none
of these things. It's the same in Stalingrad —
pears, onions, carrots, tomatoes, red peppers,
radishes in the market but not in the stores.

This is not only a matter of agricultural short-
ages, but also of distribution. State collections
from the farms go first to the privileged classes,

hotels and canteens in factories; the stores get fairly low priority.

State prices for food and most other things are very high in relation to incomes which on the average have been reckoned at 600-650 rubles ($150-$162.50) a month. So how are people able to pay the inflationary higher prices for free market food or black market goods?

For one thing, of course, many people make much more than the average. A top retail executive can make as much as 6,000 rubles ($1,500) a month, and there are plenty of executives and bureaucrats in the Soviet Union.

Then too, in a great many families more than one member works. Rents are generally low. Medical care is free. Meals in factory canteens are cheap; you can get a full-course dinner in the canteen of the Likhachev Auto Plant in Moscow for the ruble equivalent of between 88 cents and $1.28. Also, there has been such a scarcity of consumer goods for so many years that money has accumulated in people's hands.

In any case, there is plainly more money than goods about. What are the signs that this inflationary condition will worsen?

A new and more liberal pension law went into effect October 1; it's expected to pump an additional 25 billion rubles (over $6.2 billion) a year into the purchasing power stream. (No figures on total ruble circulation are available.) A minimum wage law is scheduled to go into effect January 1, adding some 32 billion rubles ($8 billion) worth of inflationary pressure. At the same time, the work week is to be reduced from 46 to 41 hours, which can hardly be expected to increase productivity as a counterbalance to inflation.

And on top of all these new pressures, Minister of Trade D. V. Pavlov says the government plans to start instalment buying in stores, perhaps next year, on big items like furniture. Extensive military activity in the Middle East or elsewhere would be a further inflationary strain, even though the Soviet Union already maintains a huge military machine.

How does the government try to counteract inflation?

The answer the planners give is that everything is planned for. When it was decided to boost pensions and minimum wages while shortening the work week, the planners figured that increased productivity would mop up the new inflationary potential. Yet the same planners concede that even by the end of the Sixth Five Year Plan (1956 through 1960), during which considerable boosts in consumer goods output are foreseen, there still won't be enough goods to meet the needs of the people.

"The trouble," says one observer, "is that the Soviets are always making plans on the basis of increased productivity, but the increases never come up to their expectations."

Theoretically, the budget surplus is an anti-inflationary force. This year's budget shows revenues of over 591 billion rubles (about $148 billion), expenditures of 568 billion ($142 billion), making a surplus of over 23 billion (about $6 billion).

But students of the Soviet system take this surplus with a large grain of salt. They detect various gimmicks, such as finding an item to cover increased procurement costs showing up on both sides of the ledger. Some suspect the surplus is largely or even wholly fictitious — which would not, however, necessarily mean the budget is in the red.

Income taxes could be jacked up, but this is not how the Soviets usually operate. Direct taxes — income and the so-called bachelor's tax on people without children — bring in only 50 billion rubles of this year's 591 billion-plus receipts. The biggest chunk of revenue comes from the turnover tax, imposed between production and distribution; it accounts for 270 billion rubles of

revenue this year. The state's share of the profits
of enterprise — in effect, a corporate profit tax
— brings in another 107 billion.

The actual rates of personal income taxes are
low — 1½%, starting on incomes of 370 rubles a
month under the new minimum wage law, to
13%. In addition, however, Soviet citizens must
pay what amounts to a tax in the form of buying
bonds, with the chance of winning prizes. These
purchases now take about a month's wages a
year. The budget expects bond buying to bring
in 32 billion rubles, maybe more, this year, of
which about 14 billion will be repaid in prizes
and interest.

The Soviets do use these forced loans as an inflationary or deflationary device. In 1954, under
former Premier Malenkov's new deal for the consumer, they halved the amount of purchase re-
quired. The result was so inflationary that they
restored the obligatory purchases to four weeks'
wages.

Part of the anti-inflation effort is a big propaganda campaign to get people to save money.
Many small savings banks have been opened, in
factories and stores as well as in buildings of
their own. Advertisements appear on bulletin
boards and hoardings in the streets of Soviet
cities. Bank representatives visit workers in fac-

tories and flats. "Save your money and build a dacha (country cottage)," is the theme.

To see that savings are in fact rising, talk to Ivan Belanski, manager of one of the seven central savings banks in Stalingrad. On January 1, 1954, the bank had 32,471 depositors with over 53.8 million rubles on deposit. On October 1, 1956, there were 48,777 depositors with 94.1 million rubles on deposit. Accounts usually pay 2% interest per year and depositors can withdraw at will.

For the Soviet Union as a whole, the current budget sees a rise of five billion rubles in savings this year to a total of 58 billion. Last year's rise was also about five billion.

It is questionable how effective an anti-inflationary force the growth of savings really is. The increase in savings is counted as revenue in the budget; yet the planners say they do not technically regard it as part of capital formation, which they consider derives chiefly from the profits of state industry and state (not collective) farms, and to a much lesser extent from the state loans. They imply, however, that since it is possible to tell on the average the amount needed to cover withdrawals from savings accounts, at least part of the savings can be used for capital investment.

In any case, many people clearly use their savings accounts not so much for long-term saving as for short-term needs. They put money in the account until they have accumulated enough to buy a big item like a refrigerator or to finance a vacation and then they clean out the account. To the extent this is the practice, the inflationary potential is not much diminished.

A big anti-inflationary control mechanism is the price structure itself. Official prices are high to begin with, even though there have been six general annual price reductions since the war. The revealing thing is that no general reduction came through either last year or this year.

The failure to decree a cut last year probably reflected an attempt to stem the big inflationary flood unloosed by the new look of 1953 and 1954. The lack of such a reduction this year is probably an effort to restrain the anticipated new flood which will come in the wake of the boosts in pensions and minimum wages. The planners, however, vigorously deny any intention of ever actually raising prices.

Finally, the government has an extreme deflationary tool at its disposal — currency reform through which the money is devalued and savings wiped out. The Soviets employed this drastic weapon in the early post-war years, and they could do it again if the inflation became serious enough.

When that happens it means, of course, that inflation has got out of control. Yet, because the state is totalitarian and relatively independent of popular feeling, observers do not believe it would have the same economic and political significance as in a Western country. They feel the state can always devalue as a last resort without necessarily ruining the economy or imperiling the political structure.

Instead, these observers see Soviet inflation as a vitiating force, constantly chewing away at productivity gains and leading to hidden price increases as when lower quality goods are sold at prices originally set for higher quality ones. This debilitating influence, they note, is serious enough by itself, even if inflation never reaches the runaway stage.

And they do not see a great deal the Soviets can do about it as long as this remains, by political decree, a scarcity consumer economy.

10...

Sightseeing, Anyone?

"WELL," says your interpreter, "we can always go sightseeing." And a visiting reporter has good reason to wonder, during his first days here, whether he will ever see anything but tourist sights.

Reporting in this country is difficult for anybody, including Soviet newspapermen. It is difficult for American and other non-Soviet correspondents on regular tours of duty here, even though the Press Office of the Ministry of Foreign Affairs recognizes their status and in theory helps them. And for a reporter just on a trip of several weeks, there are a couple of special complexities.

The basic problem is that such a reporter can come to the Soviet Union only on a "tourist" basis, which means that during his stay he is in the charge of Intourist, the travel agency. The Press Office of the Foreign Ministry may or may not help him; it has no obligation to do so. Intourist, on the other hand, while providing very good service from a tourist standpoint, has no obligation to assist the reporter in his journalistic activities.

Assuming the Press Office is uncooperative, the task becomes one of budging Intourist from its wonted ways. And that is often a head-butting-against-a-stone-wall task. The instinctive reaction of Intourist is to express grave doubt about the feasibility of any request or else pronounce it flatly impossible; at first the reporter is told, for example, that he can't visit any factory at all in the Moscow area.

True, high officials of Intourist, as well as of the Press Office of the Foreign Ministry, promise cooperation. But they also explain the difficulties, and the explanations do have a certain plausibility.

Thus the officials note that Intourist has no power to insist that a factory manager receive a visitor and that some managers are getting increasingly reluctant to do so because of the disruption of work schedules. As for visiting a Russian home, "you can't just go knock on a stranger's door and expect him to let you in," one official says. "But if," he adds, "someone invites you, that's a different matter."

Why not bypass all this officialdom? It can be done to some extent. Even a smattering of Russian helps a reporter operate independently on occasion; the more he knows, the less dependent he need be on the government. But there is a definite limit to such freedom. It would be impossible to make an impromptu visit to a factory, farm or bank and expect to get in — anything of that sort has to be arranged in advance.

The upshot of the first few days in Moscow is success on about a third of the requests, no dice on the rest. The reporter decides it is time to get on to other Soviet cities in the hope that the journalistic climate will improve once he is away from the capital.

But the jousting with Intourist recurs almost everywhere. In Tiflis things are arranged fairly expeditiously, but Stalingrad is painfully slow. You have to prod the local Intourist people for a day and a half to set up a visit to the big tractor plant. At one point you deliver a heated little lecture about the distinction between a reporter and a tourist. "But you have tourist documents," is the bland retort. Anyway, whether or not because of the exchange of words, the tractor plant tour is arranged almost immediately thereafter.

Kiev, in the Ukrainian breadbasket, seems a logical enough place from which to visit a collective farm. But it doesn't seem logical to the Soviets; no Kiev collective for you, though you get to see the Kiev State Swine Farm. When you finally visit a collective, it is outside of Leningrad, arranged on the spur of the moment after you have been told it absolutely can't be arranged.

Back in Moscow, it becomes possible to see the auto factory that was out of the question three weeks earlier. All this time the Press Office of the Foreign Ministry has supposedly been trying to get appointments for the visiting reporter with various high government officials. Nothing happens, despite constant checking with the Press Office.

When, however, you finally write the officials directly (Intourist delivers the letters but refuses to try in any other way to help arrange the interviews), you get prompt results from at least a couple of them. No reply from Communist Party Secretary Khrushchev or First Deputy Premier Mikoyan, but then they are rather busy with Poland, Hungary and the Middle East.

In the end you have to admit that Intourist — in a slow, frustrating and sometimes infuriating way — has done most of the things you have asked. Anyway, the difficulty is not with Intourist but with the failure of the government to make any agency clearly responsible for the visit-

ing reporter. The government evidently prefers
it that way.

How useful is a trip on such a basis? Plainly
it is a guided tour in effect. The farms and factories, it can be taken for granted, are among the
best the Soviets have. The ordinary people you
interview are aware that they are talking through
an interpreter who is a representative of the
state.

It's no great problem, though, to counterbalance any impressions the government may wish
to inculcate in this way. Soviet statistics themselves will tell you that by no means all farms
are as mechanized as the ones you visited. Soviet
citizens themselves will discuss various economic
"short-comings."

Moreover, you can move about on your own in
any city, and even if you do little more than observe you can still observe plenty. Sometimes you
may be able to outwit your guides, diverting
them into paths they did not intend. And there
is always luck, such as having someone invite you
to his home when you had about abandoned
hope that would ever happen.

As for the standard of living and a general feel
of the life, the government could not let you into
the country in the first place and expect to con-
ceal it. The cramped housing, the shabby clothes

and the inadequate supply of consumer goods are apparent on every hand.

Aside from showing you, in general, the better things of Soviet life, there is little or no overt attempt to propagandize the visiting reporter. Various people may try to mislead you on this or that point, but they don't try to convert you. Usually the Intourist guides, who are courteous and extremely helpful in all ways except journalistic, don't talk politics unless you start it.

Nor was there any attempt, in this case at least, to tail the reporter when he was moving on his own or to examine his bags when he was out of his hotel room. Indeed, baggage and briefcase were not inspected even on entering or leaving the country.

It's hardly an ideal situation for a reporter. But if he is willing to do some verbal battling on occasion, he can see a good deal more than he really expected.

11...

The Compleat Tourist

CARE TO BASK in the sun this winter at Sochi or Sukhumi on the Black Sea "Riviera?" Or perhaps a Volga River trip next summer? Or maybe just a week or two of puttering around the cathedrals, museums and art galleries of Leningrad and Moscow?

The appeal of these and other Soviet tourist lures may well be dimmed or destroyed by strife in Hungary and the Middle East. Still, the Soviet Union is having its biggest tourist year since World War II, and officials confidently predict a much greater influx of foreigners in 1957 and thereafter.

What's it actually like getting around this country, and how is the traveler treated?

Aside from the fact that the Russians don't cope with the weather any better than other people, it's suprisingly painless to move around — to the comparatively few places the Soviet government is willing to let you move. And considering that the official dollar-ruble exchange rate is highly disadvantageous to the dollar, the Soviets make a sojourn here relatively inexpensive.

Touring the U.S.S.R. is nonetheless a distinct change of pace, as you realize the moment you first get on a plane of the Soviet airline, Aeroflot (you can take one to Moscow from Prague, Czechoslovakia, among other places). The plane is a two-engine IL-12 based on the Douglas DC-3, which the Soviets received in quantity during Lend-Lease days. Painted on the wings and fuselage in big letters are CCCP (USSR).

This is the standard Soviet passenger plane, the only type you are likely to ride. The new four-jet job is said to be used on some eastern runs, and recently the Soviet press announced the inauguration of jet service three times a week from Moscow to Prague. But when a tourist tried to book a jet flight to Prague, Aeroflot told him there was no such service. Presumably it's still in the trial-run stage.

Inside, the IL-12 is neatly enough painted in gray and pastel blue, but the upholstery and carpets are shabby. The stewardess, who speaks a little English — very little — is a pretty, not too buxom blonde in a black skirt, white blouse and red sweater. Soviet stewardesses don't wear uniforms, and the other crew members are also haphazard on this score.

The stewardess first distributes magazines like Krokodil, the satiric weekly, and Ogonek (Little Fire), a general fact-fiction-picture weekly. No gum or mints to relieve ear pressure. In the late afternoon she serves tea in glasses with metal holders and pastries prepared in Prague. Nobody bothers to fasten his seat belt on take-off or landing.

This flight into the Soviet Union is elegant compared with later flights entirely within the country. It is the only time food of any kind is provided; even when radio trouble holds up the Kiev-Leningrad plane for two hours in Minsk — making the trip last from 9:20 a. m. till 4 p. m. — no lunch appears.

And on the Rostov-Kiev flight the IL-12 is really an antique, in the cabin at least. The wood floor is bare and badly scuffed, with only a beat-up runner down the aisle. There is no stewardess, no magazines, no gum, no seat belts. There are only nine seats altogether; the back part of the cabin has parallel wooden ledges hinged so as to lift up to accommodate cargo.

Usually these planes have a simple dashboard for the edification of passengers, near the door to the cockpit; it consists of altimeter, clock and cabin temperature gauge. On this plane there is an altimeter but no thermometer, and the place for the clock is an empty hole.

All the same, it's hard to quarrel with the ability of Russian pilots, except perhaps that they have a tendency to set you down rather abruptly.

For first-class passengers, trains and ships are comfortable and pleasant. The Red Arrow Express (it's painted blue) pulls smoothly out of Leningrad's Moscow Station right on the dot at 11:50 p.m. for the overnight trip to Moscow. This is the best train the Soviets have, and they are very proud of it.

The compartment, for two, is richly furnished in an old-fashioned way, with blue velour drapes and burnished woodwork. It has an upper and a lower berth, a small table with lamp and an armchair across from the lower berth by the window. There is a washroom for each two compartments, but no soap and no individual toilets. The usual train instructions are in German as well as Russian.

If you are lucky enough not to draw a roommate on the Red Arrow, you find plenty of space in the compartment to stretch your legs. The train has no diner, but there is a buffet from which waitresses come to your compartment in the morning selling apples and rolls. The sleeping

car porter will also bring you morning tea in the
usual glass.

Accommodations on the steamer which plies
the Volga-Don Canal between Stalingrad and
Rostov-on-Don are about on a par with the Red
Arrow, though the cabin, for one person, is of
course larger, and there is an agreeable lounge
fore and dining room aft.

Even when weather fouls up travel schedules,
the results have a peculiarly Russian accent. Thus
when the departure of the Moscow-Tiflis plane
is delayed from 3:50 a. m. to 11 a. m., you grab
a few hours' sleep in the Moscow Airport Hotel
— in a small room with four cots, two of which
are already occupied. And if a storm strands a
ship for a couple of days at a landing station in
the middle of the Volga-Don Canal there is no
alternative transportation to extricate the stuck
tourist.

Hotels are somewhat somber affairs with lob-
bies often almost bare of furniture. But that you
can find in any country, and the actual accommodations are relatively luxurious, again assuming you are traveling the most expensive way;
you usually get a two-room suite of sitting room
and bedroom plus bath. Chances are the rooms
will be furnished in what might be called Vic-
torian Russian or else 1915 Modern.

In just about any city the hotel room walls will be adorned with large paintings of the bears-playing-around-a-tree-stump school. These are hung close to the ceiling; from the top they project forward into the room, since otherwise you would have a hard time seeing them. But at least they are not political art, which is what greets you in almost all other buildings; even a doctor's treating-room is graced by a big portrait of Lenin, which somehow doesn't do much to enhance the antiseptic atmosphere or lift the patient's spirits.

A fascinating objet d'art, found in hotels in two different cities, is a stone owl on the night-table. Inside is a light bulb, so that in the dark the owl's eyes and part of the body give off a reddish glow — just the thing to lull the traveler to sleep.

Hotel bathrooms mostly creak or leak or gurgle in one place or another, and they tend to be unhandy, though this also is not an exclusively Russian trait. Showers, when there are any, are not the stall type but little gadgets which you have to hold. Soap, which you often have to ask for, doesn't lather much at best.

The Moscow tourist restaurants, in hotels like the National and Metropole, are gloomy once-ornate caverns; the Metropole restaurant is full of pillars and plants. The National offers the best

service, though it has been well said that it is all
but impossible to get a quick lunch (or breakfast
or dinner) in Moscow, or any other Soviet city
for that matter.

The Tiflis, Georgia, hotel restaurant is perhaps
the cheeriest on the tourist run, not because of
the decor but because of the people. In the afternoon and evening it's usually full of shirt-sleeved
Georgians eating and drinking great quantities of
wine and beer and generally enjoying themselves.
The waiters constantly urge you to try some
Georgian specialty like chukhirtma, a spicy chick-
en soup containing big hunks of chicken which
have to be eaten with knife and fork after the
soup has been spooned.

The orchestra in the Tiflis restaurant consists
of piano, violin, oboe and accordion, and it plays
gypsy-like tunes very loudly. Though most of the
other Soviet tourist restaurants have orchestras
of one sort or another, there is usually no place
for dancing. And only the restaurant in Leningrad's Hotel Europe, with its round tables and
red plush chairs and soft lights, really looks like
a restaurant in a Western nation.

Russian cuisine is justly famous, of course, but
something seems to have happened to it under the Communists. You can get better beef
Stroganov in New York City than you can in

Moscow, better borscht in Washington than in Leningrad, and better shishkabab in San Francisco than in Oriental-flavored Tiflis.

Hotel food here is heavy, with a disconcerting tendency to greasiness. The Soviets also have an addiction to "garnished" dishes, which means lots of tired canned peas and carrots and other oddments in addition to masses of fried potatoes. Soup is usually served in huge bowls, and if you have it first you aren't likely to have much interest in the entree.

Tipping is a problem, here perhaps more than elsewhere. Some waiters and porters, presumably clinging to the tradition of socialist equality, will refuse your money, but others will take it gladly. And except in the best Moscow hotels, it's well to be careful in your instructions to a bootblack; otherwise you may find that your cordovan oxfords have been polished, apparently with paint, a bright orange. It doesn't remove easily.

But the inconveniences are minor, and they are more than made up for by the service provided by Intourist, the Soviet travel agency founded in the mid-Twenties. An agency of the Ministry of Foreign Trade, Intourist meets your plane or train when you first arrive and thereafter is your guide, servant and nursemaid. You stay in Intourist hotels, eat in Intourist hotel restaurants; Intourist will order theatre tickets for you, take you shopping and, of course, show you the sights.

When you travel between Soviet cities, Intourist arranges all your hotel accommodations, makes all your train, plane or ship reservations and gets all your tickets, takes you to the airport or depot and meets you at the destination; the traveler can just forget about such tiresome details. Also, your luggage is whisked off the plane or train almost before you know it; perhaps in no other country can you make a faster getaway from an airport.

In addition, if you go deluxe class, Intourist provides you with a private car, chauffeur and interpreter any time you want them. The car is frequently a Zim limousine (it looks like an American car of several years back, with discernible traces of the 1947 Buick and the 1954 Pontiac), but occasionally it is a Zil (formerly the Zis, this is the Soviet Union's biggest, a replica of the 1942 Packard) or a fairly tiny Pobeda. In Moscow alone, Intourist has more than 120 cars and buses.

Though there doesn't seem to be any rigid rule about it, Intourist may send a Moscow interpreter, usually female, with the traveler wherever he goes in the country. This may sound like a gimmick for keeping the closest tabs on the tourist, and perhaps it is. Still, the traveling interpreter is a big help in a country where few speak anything but Russian or the regional language. Outside of Moscow you may thus find three people in attendance — Moscow interpreter, local guide-interpreter and chauffeur.

The charge for all this food, lodging and service is $30 a day deluxe class. It does not include drinks, theatre tickets, cigarets, laundry and other personal expenses, or transportation between cities. Below deluxe class, at cheaper rates, are superior, first, second and third classes, but persons traveling alone or in groups of less than four are required by the Soviets to travel deluxe.

If you go to Russia from the U. S., the $30 a day is prepaid in dollars for the duration of your stay before the Soviet visa is actually issued. In return for it you get a book of vouchers which you surrender for meals, hotels and intracity transportation.

It is difficult to estimate what this food, lodging and service would cost if you had to pay as you go in 25-cent rubles (official rate), but Soviet prices in general suggest it would be a lot more. A small laundry (which you do have to pay extra for) consisting of a couple of shirts and handkerchiefs and a few pairs of socks comes to

16 rubles or $4. The charge for pressing one suit and pair of slacks translates at almost $3.30. A box of good cigarets costs $1.25 or more for 20.

And here is an idea of what you would otherwise have to pay for a dinner in an Intourist restaurant: Caviar, 13.35 rubles; borscht, 7.55; ham in Madeira sauce, 10.80; coffee with cream, 2.80. That's over $8.60 for one person. A modest portion of vodka first and a beer with dinner would add about $3.75 to the bill. If you want to get away from the Intourist restaurant and are willing to pay rubles, you can get quite a good dinner at the Prague restaurant, sometimes called Moscow's 21 Club, for about $11, though you can also pay much more.

Actually the $30 a day works out at $23.75, because Intourist is now giving the tourist 25 rubles ($6.25) a day spending money. How far this goes depends on your fondness for Russian ballet, vodka and cigarets. But it certainly helps.

Transportation between cities is also fairly easy on the wallet; the Russians are currently giving the tourist a 50% reduction on such travel. A trip of about 5,000 miles within the U.S.S.R. came to less than $280.

The Russians can be hazy about these things, however. When the bill for this journey was first presented it came to over $600. The tourist

protested, the figures were double-checked and
the result was less than half the original. Apparently — at least for one thing — the 50% reduction
had not been calculated the first time.

Does such an amount really cover the ruble
cost? And does the $30 a day — or $23.75 — cover
the liberal use of manpower and gasoline? These
are questions you are not likely to get answered
in Moscow. But since the ruble is rubbery and
the dollar hard, the chances are that the dollar
exchange is worth to the Soviets more than whatever amount of rubles they have to spend to
get it.

The tourists, at any rate, have been flocking
here, comparatively speaking, from all over.
Giorgi Stankovitch, chief of Intourist's interpreter section, figures the full year 1956 may see a
total of 125,000 or more, as much as two and a
half times the number last year. At the peak
last summer Intourist was finding it hard to provide enough hotel rooms and interpreters.

But the agency is busily expanding for what
Mr. Stankovitch expects to be much bigger years
in the future; next year he thinks there might be
three times as many tourists as this year. A new
2,000-room hotel, the Ukraine, is building in Moscow, and other new ones are going up here and
in Stalingrad, Kiev, Sochi and Sukhumi.

12...

Stalin's Legacy

No One has to be told that the Soviet Union faces unresolved political and economic problems of the first magnitude. But if a sojourn here does nothing else it suggests a certain amount of caution about concluding that these problems are necessarily insoluble.

One fundamental problem is the succession of power in a state whose government does not depend on popular choice. Another is the "colonial" question — the future course with the satellites. Still a third is the allocation of resources in an economy run by the state instead of by the market.

As to the first, Soviet history is full of the gory consequences of the inability to hand on authority through any dependable political mechanism. The death of Stalin seemed to open a new era of violent struggle for one-man control, and Beria did in fact make the bid almost immediately. Within a few months of Stalin's death he was behind bars and in less than a year he had been executed.

That was, indeed, a naked struggle for power. The subsequent fall of Malenkov as Premier, the rise of Khrushchev to the Stalin-like eminence of First Secretary of the Communist party, the ouster of Molotov as Foreign Minister — all these seemed to be further reflections of clashing ambitions for the role of absolute dictator.

It is possible, however, that such an interpretation is too simple and too superficial. The fact is that since Beria no one of the top men has been liquidated or even lost any substantial power. Malenkov and Molotov remain imposing figures in the Soviet hierarchy even though they no longer have the titles they once had. By the same token, it is unlikely that Khrushchev has now or ever has had Stalin's power even though he holds one of Stalin's offices.

One theory is that none of these men was individually strong enough to draw into his hands the total authority exercised by Stalin. Not even Beria, with his huge MVD army, was able to do it.

Some observers believe that, with the exception of Beria, none even wanted to become a new Stalin. These men were, after all, the intended

victims of Stalin. They had every reason to loathe
not only the dictator but the type of dictatorship
he represented. In this view, they had to cling together and they had to act swiftly and decisively
when a man like Beria threatened to become a
new Stalin.

If these assumptions — and they are only that
— have any validity, then the shifts of power
within the Kremlin may be less significant than
they seem. Instead of a situation in which each
member of the Communist Party Presidium is
constantly plotting to do each other one in the
eye, there may be something approximating committee rule.

That is, the members of the Presidium may
enjoy about equal power and jointly select one
man — either the Premier or the Party Secretary
— as their spokesman in chief. The change of
spokesmen from time to time would then reflect
not so much palace purges as changing emphases
in national policy decided by the group as a
whole.

This, of course, is roughly the way the Soviets
say it is, when they talk about collective leader-
ship. But the fact that the Soviets say it works
this way does not automatically prove that it
works some other way.

Assuming the Soviets want committee rule,

what is to prevent a new Stalin arising to wreck it? Even if the rulers of today are on guard against that danger, the leaders of tomorrow may be less vigilant; the Soviet system by its nature is an open invitation to a resourceful, ruthless and overweeningly ambitious man.

All that can be said for sure is that it hasn't happened yet and that it is not a foregone conclusion. Fortunately, as someone has remarked, men like Stalin don't grow on trees. There is at least the possibility that self-perpetuating committee rule, even if punctuated by power struggles from time to time, could emerge as the long-run pattern. The longer it were able to operate, presumably, the more secure it would become and the less vulnerable to new would-be Stalins.

Another threat to committee rule is that it presupposes some loosening of control. Thus the policy of liberalization may have been decided upon partly because it was impossible to continue full-blown Stalinism, even if anyone wanted to, without having a Stalin running things.

The danger is that once liberalization starts, it may go much further than the rulers intend. In the Soviet Union itself, however, it would seem that the levers of control — through the Communist party and other organizations and through the security police — are still sufficiently strong to prevent matters from getting out of hand, even though signs of disaffection may mount in the coming months.

In the satellite states, on the other hand, this loosened control is having what appear to be disastrous effects from the Soviet viewpoint. The "colonial" problem, it seems plain now, would have grown acute no matter what the form of the regime in the Kremlin, but the Kremlin's policy of liberalization greatly accelerated the nationalist movement.

Perhaps the Soviets will be unable to keep the satellites in the future except at gunpoint. But it should be remembered that as a matter of national policy it is not the paramount Soviet interest to run the satellites with the iron hand of a Stalin. That did, indeed, have disastrous results — economic ruin and the paralysis of initiative.

The real Soviet interest is to have allied governments, not necessarily slaves, on its borders. If, after Hungary has been crushed, the Soviets can stabilize the satellite situation on the model of Poland — a degree of internal autonomy coupled with allegiance to the Soviet Union in most foreign matters — the chances are they would not be too displeased.

The question is whether the Soviets can stabilize the satellites in this way. As of now, however,

that question has not been finally answered in
the negative.

The future of the Soviet political system, at
any rate, will depend in no small degree on the
evolution of the Soviet economy. Today, when
you observe the dearth and inferiority of consumer goods, the antiquated aspects of some
phases of agricultural and industrial production,
the oppressive and inefficient bureacracy, it is
easy to be contemptuous of this economy.

Here again, though, caution is in order. The
Soviet economy obviously does not work remote-
ly as well as a free system, but it cannot be con-
tended that it doesn't work at all. It has not yet,
at any rate, produced such insupportable imbal-
ances as to bring it to the point of collapse —
though Stalin's political terror was bringing it
near stagnation.

One reason that the Soviet economy "works"
is that the rulers are flexible enough to leaven
it with traces of the market system, or perhaps
one should say they are incapable of eliminating
all traces. This shows up not only in such plain
cases as free markets for the produce collective
farmers grow on their private allotments, but also
in retailing and to some extent in production.

The scarcity of consumer goods, moreover, is
the result of conscious political decisions which,

in the view of the Soviet leaders, have paid enormous dividends. In the early days of Soviet rule there were those who wanted to give consumer goods the lion's share of investment, but the decision was to emphasize producer goods instead.

The proponents of heavy industry argued that only thus could the Soviets build a huge military machine and at the same time produce enough steel, oil and electric power to make this a leading industrial nation. Today they can look back and say that if they had emphasized consumer goods instead, the Soviet people might be better clothed and otherwise richer in material things, but the Soviet Union would be a sixth or fifth ranking power instead of the second power in the world; indeed, they can contend, it probably would have been crushed by Hitler in World War II.

There is, plainly enough, an answer to this argument. If this resources-rich country could have had a free-market, consumer-based economy it might well be economically much stronger today than it is — able, like the United States, to afford both guns and butter. But since that would have meant a renunciation of Communist economics it was unthinkable.

It does not seem likely, in any event, that the Soviets will any time soon "sacrifice" heavy in-

dustry for the sake of consumer goods. Even under Malenkov's premiership the argument in the
Presidium turned not on the question of actually
cutting back heavy industry but on the more
subtle and less vital question of slowing the rate
of development of heavy industry somewhat in
order to permit more consumer production, and
even on this the vote went against slowing the
heavy industry rate. Presumably to underscore
this decision, Malenkov was let out as Premier,
though not out of power.

As long as the priority goes to heavy industry,
the basic economic problem of allocating resources is manageable if not simple; in effect,
such investment as is left over from heavy industry goes to agriculture and consumer goods. Year
by year, however, the volume of consumer output is growing even though its percentage of
total production may remain static; the whole
industrial base of the Soviet Union, in other
words, is expanding.

That means that the problem of allocating resources, which is more or less automatically
solved by the market in a free economy, is be-
coming more serious for the totalitarian planners.
If the time ever comes when the Soviets cut back
substantially on military production, the difficulty
of deciding how much to allocate for shoes

against purses, refrigerators against washing machines, could become hair-raising.

Perhaps, in that case, part of the answer will
be a still greater leavening of the Soviet system
with the yeast of the market economy. Once such
a process got going, it could have incalculable
political as well as economic consequences. A
degree of economic freedom plus rising living
standards could create a popular mood which
might force the leaders to moderate their political controls still further.

But that is looking far ahead, and perhaps
looking too wishfully at that. As of now the problems of transferring power, of dealing with the
satellites, of allocating resources — and these of
course do not exhaust the list of headaches — remain basic and unsolved. And the fixations of
Communist ideology are formidable obstacles to
any significant liberalizing of the Soviet political
and economic system.

All the same, a traveler in these parts is likely
to begin to question the assumption that the
Soviet system is capable of moving only in the
direction of rigidity and repression until it finally
collapses of its own dead weight.